Buddhism is a major influence in British thought these days through the New Age Movement and postmodernism, the spread of yoga and meditation etc. I rejoice in a clear book of this sort which relates to it. This simple and genuine story should be read by any Christians who face the issues of Eastern religions.
Martin Goldsmith

Esther's story is a beautiful one, an accounting of Christ's shepherding hand, as she is led out from under a deeply blinding idolatry and into his eternal life-giving light and tender love. She had long searched for truth, and once in Truth's presence, awed and obedient in him, she opens her entire being to the fullness of meaning and being that he alone can give. And what a blessing it is to see how she is faithfully, on some of the most difficult of mission fields, passing this miracle on to the neediest of others. In doing so, she treads in the long train of all those who 'hold to the testimony of Jesus' and worship him (Rev. 19:10), while passing on their testimony (the saving gospel!) to others.
Leanne Payne

I thoroughly endorse this book. It is full of exciting stories and I would highly recommend it to all seekers of the truth and all who long to see if Jesus is real today.
Jackie Pullinger

A gripping story of one woman's journey from Buddhist nun to faith in Jesus Christ. Deeply respectful to adherents of both faiths, it portrays positively a conclusion of Christian joy.
Laurence Singlehurst

I once was a Buddhist Nun

Esther Baker

ivp

INTER-VARSITY PRESS
Norton Street, Nottingham NG7 3HR, England
Email: *ivp@ivpbooks.com*
Website: *www.ivpbooks.com*

First published 2009

British Library Cataloguing in Publication Data
A catalogue record for this book is available from the British Library.

ISBN: 978-1-84474-384-1

Set in 11.5/14 Chaparral
Typeset in Great Britain by CRB Associates, Potterhanworth, Lincolnshire
Printed in Great Britain by Ashford Colour Press Ltd, Gosport, Hampshire

Inter-Varsity Press publishes Christian books that are true to the Bible and that
communicate the gospel, develop discipleship and strengthen the church for its
mission in the world.

Inter-Varsity Press is closely linked with the Universities and Colleges Christian
Fellowship, a student movement connecting Christian Unions in universities
and colleges throughout Great Britain, and a member movement of the
International Fellowship of Evangelical Students. Website: *www.uccf.org.uk*

Hell . . . is an image of an unchanging state which endures no more becoming.[1]

Contents

Acknowledgments

The writing and publication of this book has truly been a team effort. You are too many to mention by name, but each one of you knows who you are. It would have lacked something special without you being part of it, so I would like to thank everyone involved. What a wonder it has been to watch it unfold together! 'The LORD has done this, and it is marvellous in our eyes' (Psalm 118:23).

* * *

Although this is a true story, some of the names of people and places have been changed, including the author's.

* * *

My perspective on the Buddhist faith comes from my experience of the Theravada tradition. Other modes of Buddhism have different beliefs and practices from those described in this book.

Foreword

Sometimes the best guides to discovering Jesus Christ are those who can articulate the darkness they have walked in and their revelation of the true Light.

Esther Baker is one such guide. In recounting her earnest yet misdirected quest for truth as a Buddhist nun, Esther gently exposes the deception of Eastern mysticism; more than that, she reveals the unfailing love of God revealed to her in Christ.

Esther's profound conversion grants her that authority. In recounting her story, she manifests a fullness of grace and truth that invites us all to discover Jesus afresh.

Whether or not our starting point is Buddhism makes no difference. Esther makes clear that Christ is the goal, one that all can attain. She convinces us that he comes to us, not through our strenuous religious effort, but through the power of his great obedience.

His faithful love to her is his faithful love to each of us. I especially like the way Esther recounts the role that many different Christians played in her conversion. Each played a specific role in manifesting Jesus to her in a way that exposed the inadequacy of Buddhist tradition and in turn the fullness of Jesus.

Let Esther's story manifest Jesus afresh to you. Let the transforming love that changed her life beautifully do the same for you.

Andrew Comiskey
Author and Founder/Director of Desert Stream Ministries

1 Rock bottom

'Peace I leave with you; My peace I give to you. Let not your heart be troubled neither let it be afraid.'
(John 14:27 NKJV)

It was the morning of Sunday 21 July 1991, a warm summer's day. The wind-battered hilltop was today pleasantly bathed with a sunny glow. I was living in a Buddhist monastery, north of London, England. In bad weather it often felt like a bleak place, dotted with the wooden huts in which we lived. The huts had a temporary look about them, built above the ground, which seemed to encourage nasty gusts of chilled air to blow underneath. The trees and shrubs we had planted in the field were still very young, but were beginning to add a bit more greenery to the surroundings.

We hadn't had the meal yet, but I wasn't hungry that day. I had other things on my mind. I was one of the few ordained members of the community left at the temple. Nearly everyone, including the lay people and guests staying with us, had departed early in the morning to attend an ordination ceremony at our other monastery in the south of England. This was one of the highlights of the year, our biggest ceremonial event – the one day when suitable men and women could take the higher ordination. I had relished seeing new people ordain. It was exciting and full of meaning for me. Ordinarily I would not have missed it. But this year I didn't want to be there. I had asked for permission not to go.

I had lived in a Buddhist temple for eight years, most of that time in England as a nun (although I spent the first six months in a forest temple in Thailand before ordaining). I had taken two ordinations, initially as a novice and then as a Buddhist nun (known as a ten-precept nun). I was searching deeply for truth, and had strongly believed that Buddhism could take me there. I had given up everything that was necessary to follow the Buddhist way.

Some people may consider it an extreme way to live. The life of a Buddhist nun was strict and disciplined. It involved many ascetic practices which had the aim of giving up the pleasures of the world in search for truth. They were designed to simplify life and help us detach from earthly things. Living like this was often very tiring, but it had become normal for me and very much part of me. We slept little, ate only one meal a day and experienced much sensory deprivation. We didn't listen to the radio or television, and so at some level were cut off from the world. I was known for my strong faith in Buddhism and hadn't ever really doubted the purpose of living like this. Until now.

Something had changed dramatically.

I had begun seriously to doubt Buddhism. This had never happened before and I was inwardly shaken and somewhat bewildered as a result, none of which I liked. I wanted and needed to be sure. I didn't know what was happening to me or where the strong persistent faith that I once had was disappearing to: it felt like sand slipping out of my fingers. Today I was at a peak of confusion and inner turmoil. I don't know where I was when I made the decision to go out of the temple.

Suddenly I found myself, with my shaven head and dark-brown robe, running down to the traditional Anglican church in the nearby village. It was totally spontaneous. I didn't know who or what I would find there. I just found myself tearing out of the monastery and rushing down the hill. I was aware as I went that I had asked no-one's permission to leave. This was more urgent than etiquette! I just fled. My head was in a spin. I thought, 'I've got to talk to somebody, I've got to understand what's happening to me.' I felt deep down that someone in the church would have the answer, but I had no idea who or why.

I arrived at the end of the 8.30am communion service, just as people were going home. I must have been quite a sight as I entered the church and looked round anxiously, trying to spot the vicar. I urgently needed to talk to him. When most people had left, I caught sight of him at the front, near the east end of the church, and headed straight for him. He looked like a kind, understanding, elderly man – someone I could immediately trust. 'Could you pray for me, please?' I asked without hesitation. 'I'm very confused.' Without questions, he graciously guided me to the communion rail, near the holy table, and asked me to kneel. He laid his hands on my shoulders and prayed. As he did this I broke down, sobbing uncontrollably.

Unbeknown to me, I was causing quite a stir with the regular congregation, many of whom were elderly, well-respected people from the village. They were intrigued to know what was going on, amazed that someone of my appearance had come to talk to the vicar. The vicar's wife discreetly fielded their questions as they left the church. She knew I was a Buddhist nun and had seen one of our Buddhist monks from the community in their church before, so she wasn't as startled as some with the unusual events of that Sunday morning.

After the tears abated, the vicar's compassionate eyes met mine, and he said, 'We need to talk.' Unfortunately, he had to go immediately to lead another service in a nearby village church and he was concerned about leaving me. So he suggested a time to meet the following Tuesday morning – nine o'clock at the vicarage. This suited me well. As much as I wanted to talk, I knew I had to get back to the monastery for the meal and didn't want to be missed.

I left the church with great hope. I felt so much better already and walked back to the temple with a spring in my step. Finally I had shared this hidden turmoil with someone and after I had been prayed for, there had been a great release of emotions and conflict deep inside me. I didn't understand what had happened, but it seemed that things were looking up. This man of God might be able to help me find some answers. I was relieved and expectant. We would meet again soon; only two days until this very special appointment. What would he say to me? Would he have the answer? Somehow I felt and hoped very much that he would. I knew I wouldn't tell anyone in the Buddhist temple about our meeting, as I feared they wouldn't understand. I would keep it to myself.

Each time I thought about it over the next couple of days, it was like a light being switched on in a dark room. How things had changed, from being so certain about my Buddhist faith, to barely being able to contain my excitement about this appointment with an Anglican vicar! The community would be back that evening. I needed to plan my strategy for escape.

2 Childhood, youth and student days

'For I know the plans I have for you,' declares the LORD, 'plans to prosper you and not to harm you, plans to give you hope and a future. Then you will call on me and come and pray to me, and I will listen to you. You will seek me and find me when you seek me with all your heart.'
(Jeremiah 29:11–13)

I was born in 1956, near Liverpool, England. My parents were living in rented accommodation at the time, my father was in the RAF, and I was the second child. My brother Derek had been born only fourteen months before, so my parents had their hands full! Our sudden appearance was quite a shock for them, especially as they had waited eight years for their first child. They had started to think that they might not be able to have children at all. Then we both appeared with great haste! Suddenly there were two little ones needing time and attention and two sets of nappies to wash and change. As we were not far apart in age, and for most of the time were a similar size, people often thought we were twins. From the beginning my brother and I were almost inseparable; where you would find one, you would usually find the other.

Mum's pregnancy with me had not been easy. At six months she started to haemorrhage badly, so she wrapped herself up in towels, went outside to the phone box and called for an ambulance. She was very afraid that she might lose the baby. She was hospitalized for ten days and during her time there a vicar came to see her and offered to pray with her. My unbelieving mum agreed. She had been told by the doctor that it might well be, when the birth came, that only one of us would survive. She was afraid and so, with the vicar's encouragement, prayed that God would save both of us, and she dedicated her baby, not knowing if I was a boy or girl, to God. She went home and took it easy for the rest of her pregnancy. Wonderfully, when she came to give birth, we both survived – both mum and baby were fine, and her prayers had been answered. At a suitable time, following the custom of the day, my parents had both my brother and me baptized.

Despite this seemingly Christian start, my parents were actually bitter towards the church and angry with it too. As a child in the 1920s, my father had been put in a rather Dickensian police orphanage not far from London, after his father had died. This was painful and confusing for him as his mother was still alive then and he couldn't understand why he wasn't living with her rather than in this dreadful orphanage. He never did get an answer. There he was hungry much of the time, missed his mother terribly, lacked real love and connection with others and was forced to go to church on Sundays to hear what he said was a hard, severe gospel message. He hated being in the orphanage and really disliked church too. His idea of getting something from the church was to steal some money from the offering bag as it was passed around, so that he could buy something to alleviate his hunger.

My mother grew up in the countryside in East Anglia, the eastern part of England. Her family lived a simple country life, but they faced many hardships and money was scarce at times. Her father was a gardener and a very dedicated church warden to the local village church, a religious, strict man but a loving father. She was forced to walk to church three times a day on a Sunday in her best clothes, with her four siblings, to worship a God whom she didn't really know or understand. It was a chore for her that built resentment towards the church, lasting much of her lifetime. In all these obligatory religious childhood activities, it seems she wasn't able to meet with the God she was there to praise and worship.

When my mum and dad met in London, just after the Second World War, my father was already married and had a two-year-old son. Dad was in quite bad shape after being one of the few gunners in the RAF who actually survived the war. Tragically, many of his companions had been killed. His nerves were shot, he was drinking heavily, was having nightmares, and had little support to help him recover from the traumas he had been through. Mum had moved to London and was working as a cook for a boys' college. They met and fell very much in love and took refuge in each other. Dad left his first wife and son and married my very beautiful, much younger mother. Mum doted on Dad and took very good care of him, feeding, comforting and nurturing him back to health. Together they started a new life in postwar London and were very happy, living a life which definitely did not include God. Trying hard to put the past behind them, they danced and partied into the future.

When I was two years old, in the late 1950s, Dad was posted to Singapore for two years and we all lived there as a family, after arriving by ship. (My stepbrother was not with us and for most of our childhood days he was out of the picture. He did come back into our lives some years later, when we learned that he had emigrated to Australia to start a new life.)

One thing that we all developed during that time was a great love and respect for the Chinese and an enjoyment of being in Asia. Mum had a lot of leisure time then and decided to go to sewing classes where some Chinese people taught her to sew, including how to make her own patterns from newspaper on the floor, which she can still do to this day. She had great joy in making many beautiful clothes both for herself and the family. Eventually, doing alterations became Mum's profession 'from home', which she did for many decades and still does now, although to a much lesser degree, in her eighties. She always talks with gratitude of the Chinese who taught her to sew.

While Mum was off doing her various leisure activities, I was left at home with a maid from Malaysia, with whom I bonded very deeply, possibly even more deeply than with my mother at that time. The maid seemed to have endless time to be with me, but Mum was often elsewhere.

At one point we left Singapore for a month-long, very happy family holiday in Hong Kong. It was amazing to see the Chinese men running about with their rickshaws, which were plentiful at the time. We have lovely family photos of my brother Derek and I standing on either side of Mum, as little three- and four-year-olds, holding onto her colourfully patterned, very full 1950s skirt, about to cross the road. This was how she 'transported' us, each one firmly attached to her skirt, completely forbidden to let go until all was safe! She had, and still has, an amazing dress sense, really enjoying bold colours and shapes in the material she chooses, and is usually turned out beautifully.

In the early 1960s we all returned to England, this time by plane.

I was a sensitive child, as was my brother, and although my parents tried their best, in their own neediness and brokenness they were not able to meet all of our needs, especially on an emotional level.

When I was six years old, we were living in an RAF camp in central England when my father was sent to Borneo to fight in the civil war. It was a difficult and dangerous assignment.

This naturally made my mum feel very vulnerable, being left at home with two little ones, and she didn't know if Dad would ever return, as there were some very real casualties to this war. Mum felt very unsafe and ill at ease.

As a result, she became very ill with a nervous condition while my father was away. She was put under medical care, and my father was brought back from Borneo to help support and take care of her. It was quite some time before she recovered and my brother and I, young as we were, had to learn not to have needs at that time. She received various forms of medical help, but in the end Mum claims that what helped her most was being put under hypnosis. I realized later on that some of these sad things that occurred in our childhood did cause some deep emotional pain for my brother and myself.

I was around seven years old when Mum started to improve. I remember she took us to a neighbour's séance. She was sometimes attracted to these strange things. Occasionally she would go to visit a palm reader or fortune teller with my auntie, while my brother and I would wait in the car. Being introduced to these things at an early age actually opened up a door of intrigue in the occult for me, which I dabbled with in my youth and early adulthood.

For years, if my dad heard a vicar's voice he would become angry. The pain of his childhood and the deep neglect that he had experienced ran deep in him, and he felt that the church had never really helped him (apart from the 'perks' from the offering bag). Together my parents nurtured their dislike for the church. I grew up in this atmosphere and naturally started to think, talk and behave similarly to them, as did my brother. 'Christians are a joke, pathetic, and Christianity is worthless rubbish,' I remember scribbling on a Bible once as a child, such little respect did I have for the Word of God, and no RE teacher – most of whom regretted having me in their class – could convince me otherwise.

(Rebellion and a strong self-will were noticeable character traits in each of my family members!)

As I grew up I prided myself on being an atheist – not that I totally understood what that meant, but certainly it spelt out to me that God was *not* in the picture. My philosophy of life then, as my dad had taught me, was to look after number one and that's what I did, as well as thinking that it was fine to do what I liked as long as I didn't affect anyone else. My early life was barren of spiritual care or interest and we all seemed quite happy with it that way.

As a child I would spend hours with Dad in the garden, following him around, which he seemed happy for me to do and which I really loved. He gave me my own special little patch in the garden, which I treasured, and he taught me how to sow vegetable seeds in it. He loved growing vegetables; he wasn't interested in flowers, as he said you couldn't eat them! This was a man who had learned to survive. He was never able to sow his carrots in a straight line, but it didn't matter as they grew anyway and we took much delight in picking and eating them.

Over the years I developed a great love of nature and gardening and decided that I wanted to go into horticulture as a career. I had the great opportunity to study at a prestigious horticultural college in London in the 1970s for three years, an amazing opportunity for an eighteen-year-old. It was challenging and exciting. Working with plants from all over the world, a desire was born in me to travel and see some of these plants in their native habitats. I really enjoyed my time there and was convinced that my life would be spent in a career in horticulture, maybe in a remote botanical garden somewhere, saving the world's rare buttercups. The opportunities were endless for those who studied at the college.

During my three years as a student in London I lived very much on my own terms. At times I could swear like a trooper and drink to excess, smoking, going to parties and having promiscuous relationships, including one-night stands. These were the 1970s: my friends and I were indulging in our new-found freedom, sexual and otherwise. We lived as if we were our own gods, often without boundaries and free – or so we thought. I developed an interest in the occult, including séances, astrology and tarot cards.

By the time I was twenty-one I was emotionally exhausted. I had 'lived hard' for three years, trying to fill up the emptiness and neediness inside me, searching for security and happiness in worldly pleasures and various lovers. It takes a lot of stamina, particularly emotionally, to live like that in the longer term and I felt exhausted, at my end and very alone. Paradoxically, living like that actually fuelled the isolation and despair rather than decreasing it. Looking after number one had taken me to a very barren place and deep inside I knew that something was going to have to change.

I remember well the prize-giving day when we were given our certificates. It was really one of the best days of my life, as amazingly I had received an honours diploma. As I couldn't bear the thought of failing, I had worked very hard, so much so that I had excelled. Would I now realize my dream of becoming a plant conservationist, perhaps on a remote tropical island, saving wild flora? That would be a wonderful and meaningful thing to do.

However, as I was standing at the gate of the college with the diploma in my hand, the thought suddenly came, 'So what?' So what, at the end of my life? Was that really it? Was that the real meaning of life, or was there more? I realized that I still had many questions, and in an instant I knew I couldn't give my life to a career in horticulture. I didn't really want what I had been working towards for so long.

So what exactly was it that I was looking for? I was truly puzzled. I needed time to think and to understand what I was feeling. The eventful journey of the search for truth was about to begin.

3 Attraction to Buddhism

[We] do not know who we are, and will search for our identity in someone or something other than God until we find ourselves in Him.
(Leanne Payne[1])

I took a break at that point. Actually I had no choice. I had no desire to pursue the career I had studied for, even though I still loved horticulture. Questions were spinning around in my head and I needed time to think. 'Who am I?' 'What's life about?' 'What happens when you die?' My spiritual side, which had been suppressed for so many years, was now erupting and demanding answers. I was desperate for answers, and that had now overtaken my desire for a career in horticulture. At twenty-one years old, the search for truth became the most important thing in my life. As a drowning person needs air, I had to find it. It became my central drive and motivation. Everything else paled into insignificance by comparison.

At least now I knew what I was looking for. This was the challenge I faced: what is this truth and how do I know it to be right, when many doctrines and religions claim to have it?

I was living in London, where a pot-pourri of spiritual options was on offer, so I went to visit various groups, including the Hare Krishnas, and listened to Jehovah's Witnesses. I tried to go to church, but couldn't cope with that as I had been so indoctrinated against it in my childhood, and eventually someone said to me, 'You sound like a Buddhist.' I had always thought that Buddhists were peaceful and compassionate, so the thought came to me, 'Perhaps I am a Buddhist, perhaps that's who I really am.' So I answered an advert in *Time Out* magazine for those interested to learn more about Buddhism, and met an English man who encouraged me to go to a temple run by a Sri Lankan Buddhist monk in north London. Soon afterwards, I found my way there.

The Buddhist monk was a patient, scholarly man who appeared to have answers to my many questions. I poured my heart out to him. He even had questions that I hadn't thought of! What he taught really did appeal to my intellect and, as Buddha did not in any way acknowledge God, I found it really easy to accept the teachings. I was very impressed with the monk and with Buddhism, and soon was attending weekly courses on Buddhism at the temple. Not long after this I was calling myself a lay Buddhist (a follower of Buddhism who is not ordained and lives an ordinary working/family life) and feeling comfortable with that. Becoming a lay Buddhist didn't involve any initiation ceremony, but in my mind it meant that I was aiming to follow the Buddha's teaching. I started to observe the five Buddhist precepts: not to destroy any life, not to steal, not to commit adultery, not to tell lies, not to take intoxicating drinks. I felt in my heart that I had found a vehicle to help me discover what I was looking for.

I did some research and I found out that Buddha was a man, born in the sixth century BC, a prince in a royal family in what was then north India, which is present-day Nepal. His personal name was Siddhattha, his family name was

Gotama. At a young age he married a beautiful princess and enjoyed a life of luxury, privilege and pleasure. His father made sure that he was never exposed to pain, suffering or death, until one day he escaped, curious to know what was outside the protective walls of his palace.

Stories tell that once outside, he travelled around and saw many things for the first time, including an old person, someone who was sick, a dead body and a monk. It is recorded that he was shocked and deeply moved when confronted with the reality of human suffering, sickness and death. After seeing these 'signs', a deep and urgent desire arose in him to find the way out of suffering. These thoughts didn't leave him and soon afterwards, at the age of twenty-nine, shortly after the birth of his only child, he escaped from the palace again to become an ascetic, one who had given up the world in search of answers.

Although our motivations were different (the Buddha's primary aim was to escape and find an end to suffering, whereas mine was to find truth), I could relate very much to Siddhattha's search. He had enjoyed privilege (and I had tried hard to find fulfilment in various worldly pleasures by that time), but still they weren't enough. Something was driving him on to find answers.

Siddhattha started his search by following the local religious teachers of the day, going through various rigorous practices such as self-denial and mortification, sometimes fasting to an extreme. This didn't provide the answers he was looking for, however, so he abandoned known methods to find his own way. By now he was extremely weak from fasting, and he gained strength by taking some food. One evening, with his focus on finding an end to suffering, he sat down under a fig tree, near a river in north India, and meditated. There he had an unusual and extreme experience which became known as 'enlightenment', after which he was known as Buddha. He was thirty-five years old. The experience under the fig tree remains the goal of Buddhism to this day.

Not long after this, Buddha started to teach the philosophical insights he had had under the tree, and before long men and women wanted to follow him. That is how the order of Buddhist monks and nuns came into being. For forty-five years he taught all kinds of people, travelling far and wide across India. He never claimed to be God, or even a little 'god', just a man. He passed away at the age of eighty, and was cremated.

I was impressed with the idea that Buddha claimed to have found truth *himself*. He said that all his insights were due to his own endeavours and human intelligence. He claimed no inspiration or help from God, indeed any god or external power, and said that each person is his or her own 'master'. In fact, he denied that God or any power sits in judgment over our destiny. As I, like my parents, didn't believe in God and found all of that rather difficult and irritating, this really made sense to me. I liked the idea of finding truth for myself.

The Buddha's goal seemed very appealing to me then. It felt like a breath of fresh air after the other extreme of self-indulgence and the resulting emotional weariness that I was eager to shake off. However, although the Buddha's goal is known by many names – such as *nirvana* (Sanskrit) and *nibbana* (depending on the country and particular Buddhist tradition) – my experience has been that not many people are aware of its true nature. Even Buddhist monks find it hard to explain. It is described as 'extinction' and 'the unconditioned', a state in which nothingness and the absence of desire or craving is the ultimate goal, the place 'where all becoming ceases'.

Another aspect of Buddha's teaching that appealed to me was his idea that the world and everything in it, whether mental or physical phenomena, are impermanent and unsatisfactory. He claimed that no-one has a self or soul; we are only bundles of changing elements of various kinds. (Paradoxically, he taught that we must depend on ourselves – a self that he said didn't exist – to find the way out of suffering.)

This idea of not having a soul ('nobody at home') rang true and felt familiar to me. I wasn't in any way depressed, but I sometimes had feelings of emptiness inside, as though I didn't know who I was or where I belonged. Buddhism was affirming me in this, teaching that there is no permanent self or ego to be found, and I was quick to embrace it. The idea of being nothing, having nothing and no-one, was more familiar and appealing at the time than the ability to rejoice in and embrace life.

In retrospect, however, I know that those feelings of emptiness are *not* who I truly am, but there were reasons why I felt like that. They had their origin in a lack of sufficient nurture, affirmation and security in my childhood (in a nutshell, a type of primal emotional deprivation) which resulted at times in a lack of well-being and uncertainty in my identity. I also know now that, just as there were causes for these feelings, there is an answer to them too: in themselves they are not the ultimate reality or truth. I see now that the teaching about not having a soul is a great error with disastrous consequences (see pp. 146–147 for a prayer for God's affirmation of your identity and inner being).

In teaching that we have no self or soul, all that is unique about each human life is in effect denied existence. As these essential parts of our humanity are not recognized or acknowledged in Buddhism, they will be overlooked and not affirmed in us. Then, of course, it becomes impossible to know who we truly are or why we were born, as we are not seeing the full picture of who we have been created to be. Looking back on this now, I think of the seed of a large tree trapped under a big stone at germination so that it can't ever reach the light: it may be alive, but it can't develop into the fullness, magnitude and wonder of what it was created to be. In denying that we have a self or soul, the inherent uniqueness, fullness and beauty of each individual life will not be able to flourish or fully express who we truly are.

In contrast to Buddhism, teaching that we have a soul and self is a core part of Christianity. It was not until much later, however, that I would read in the Bible the prayer of the apostle Paul: 'May God himself, the God of peace, sanctify you through and through. May your whole spirit, soul and body be kept blameless at the coming of our Lord Jesus Christ' (1 Thessalonians 5:23).

At the time, as my interest in Buddhism increased, I started to feel that I had found what I was looking for, something that could answer my questions, and over a period of years I became more and more interested. I read lots of Buddhist books and went on many courses and meditation retreats in various places. Even though I moved and travelled quite a bit, I always tried to live near a Buddhist temple so that I could continue my studies and develop my understanding.

I discovered that the type of Buddhism I had been learning from the Sri Lankan monk was called 'Theravada Buddhism' and is mainly found in countries such as Sri Lanka, Thailand, Burma (Myanmar), Cambodia and Laos, but there was also another type called 'Mahayana Buddhism' which can be found in places such as Tibet, Mongolia, China, Taiwan, Japan and Korea (the Dalai Lama being an example of a Tibetan monk from the Mahayana tradition).

A couple of years after becoming a Buddhist, I decided to go on a Buddhist retreat in Kathmandu, Nepal, with two Tibetan lamas (monks), studying Mahayana Buddhism for a month in 1979. This was my first retreat and first trip back to Asia since childhood. However, it didn't appeal to me in the same way that Theravada Buddhism did. I felt there was something too dark and mysterious within Tibetan Buddhism for me – I later discovered that it has other forms of the occult mixed in with it – and I felt safer with what I knew.

Although I received most of my training and teaching from the Sri Lankan monk, I had started to visit a Buddhist temple in the south of England too. This was a temple started by an American monk and was a community of mainly Western monks and nuns. He had lived in the forests of Thailand for ten years, studying under a famous Thai Buddhist meditation master. An English friend of mine who had been a supporter of the Sri Lankan monk in London had ordained there, so I went to visit her and I knew from the beginning that if ever I was to give up my ordinary life and become a Buddhist nun (in other words, become ordained), I wanted to ordain there as they seemed so dedicated and sincere. I really enjoyed being able to talk about Buddhism with Westerners who had given their lives to it. I started to feel an interest in visiting the international temple in the north-east of Thailand where many of the senior monks had lived and trained. I felt excited but very much challenged being with this community. Would it ever be possible that I could be like them?

My life was much simpler now than before: I was not drinking alcohol and I was more stable in my relationships. As a result I began to feel uncomfortable at parties. I remember going to a friend's birthday party and feeling quite awkward and disengaged, sipping my orange juice and looking for a good reason to leave! In the past I would have been the life and soul. Things had changed and I knew it. I wanted more and more just to meditate and become absorbed in the teachings of the Buddha, to withdraw and keep life simple. To 'let go' of the world, not to engage with it, brought about a kind of peace, the peace that comes from sensory deprivation, from simply not being stimulated.

As my interest in Buddhism grew, the idea of pursuing a career disappeared. It was clear that the pursuit of truth and the spiritual goal were definitely my top priorities and would remain so. I was very grateful for my studies and time at the horticultural college and often my work involved horticulture, but working had now become solely a means of support for the pursuit of truth.

My friends were now mainly Buddhists or open to Buddhist ideas, or people I met at the temple, sometimes English, sometimes Asian. I had one good Sri Lankan friend in London, a married lady with a family, and she would regularly invite me to her home on a Friday night for one of her fantastic curries. My Asian friends liked it that I was interested in Buddhism. My parents didn't realize the change that was going on in me as we generally didn't talk about our feelings and thoughts – we were not really close in that way. Nor did I feel inclined to share it with them, as I felt they wouldn't understand.

My trip to Nepal had whetted my appetite and I began to want to travel in Asia more and more. I wanted to see the effect that Buddhism had on the cultures and people of Buddhist countries. In many of those countries the language, thinking, beliefs and everyday life of the people have very much been shaped by Buddhism. So between 1980 and 1981, I spent five months travelling to different places in Asia.

First of all I went to Sri Lanka, which I had longed to visit after hearing the Sri Lankan monk I knew speak so much about it. There I travelled quite a bit and stayed in various places, such as Colombo and Kandy. I visited a number of Buddhist temples and went on my first solitary retreat for a few days in a temple. I was meditating and reading about Buddhism most of the time. Kind Sri Lankan lay people would bring me food each day, so that I didn't need to go out and be distracted. Their offerings included wonderful hot curries, rice, exotic vegetables, fruits and delicious yogurt made from buffalo milk with palm syrup to go on top. They really seemed to like having a Western woman staying with them, practising

Buddhism. Despite their kind attention, I remember that I didn't enjoy the retreat very much. I wasn't really sure how to do it and didn't have a teacher. It felt too quiet, like being in solitary confinement. I was very relieved when it was all over and I could get out and about again!

I then joined a Buddhist pilgrimage to India, the only Western woman with about thirty-five Sri Lankan Buddhists. We flew from Colombo to Madras in the south of India, then travelled north to Calcutta, Deli and later in a westerly direction towards Bombay (Mumbai). We travelled most of the time by train, living a simple life in a train carriage together for a month. We even had our own cooks who prepared food on the train, which helped to make sure it was clean. I slept in a compartment with a Sri Lankan 'auntie' and some younger girls. I was glad for the safety of living in the train: we had bars over the windows. At nearly every station beggars would come running eagerly with their hands outstretched, longing for help, especially when they saw a white face. I had never seen poverty like it. We visited the Buddhist places of interest, such as where Buddha was born, died and sat under the fig tree, and we worshipped at the various sites. My Sri Lankan friends continued on to Bombay by train, but I left them to catch a flight to go for the first time to Thailand. I planned to spend a short time in the international English-speaking temple in the north-east, where the American monk from the temple in the south of England had lived and trained. I was keen to stay there and see for myself what it was like.

I arrived in Bangkok, a bustling city, and found somewhere to stay among the tourists. It was interesting to see many Buddhist monks in their orange robes out and about in Bangkok. In England the monks and nuns I had met – both Asian and Western – had been impeccable in keeping the Buddhist monastic code, as far as I could see, whereas in Thailand I remember being shocked to see some town monks smoking and using money, which is really stretching the monastic code! But it didn't put me off.

After a short while I was relieved to leave the busy city and catch the night train up to Ubon Ratchatani, a provincial town in the north-east near the Laos border. It was amazing to travel through mile after mile of paddy fields with buffaloes, and to see the small farms and simple Thai villages. It looked as if there was poverty here too, but not on the scale that I'd seen in India. It was a long journey and made me realize what a big country Thailand is.

From the railway station I made my way out to the temple. The nuns in England had given me directions, but I was very relieved when I eventually found it! The temple was located in a natural forest, some of the trees being teak, and it was not far from a small village. It was surrounded by paddy fields.

The first thing I noticed as I entered was how cleanly the paths in the forest had been swept. I didn't see any people to begin with, but could tell that monks were living there by the cleanness of the paths. Actually, from that time on, every time I returned to the temple (which would be several times over the next few years) the first thing I would do on entering would be to check that the paths were swept, as a sign that the monks (or someone at least) were still there.

At this time there was a small community of Western monks and one or two women living there. I was glad to be able to talk to the two English women (one nun and one about to ordain), to find out more about their life and their reasons for being there. My stay was brief, however. I was very glad to have gone there, but had plans to move on and spend a short time in Japan.

It was winter when I arrived in Tokyo, just before Christmas. In Japan I felt more like a tourist. I didn't have any contacts there and wasn't very familiar with Japanese Buddhism. I travelled somewhat, went to Kyoto and looked at the Buddhist temples from the outside. I couldn't find a temple to stay in, but was glad I went none the less. It was interesting to see the different expressions of Buddhism in various countries, all of which originated, however, from the same man's teaching.

I found this trip to Asia fascinating. My commitment to Buddhism was clearly increasing. I had been a lay Buddhist for six years and started to wonder where this growing, deepening faith would lead. Gradually I started to feel more at home within a Buddhist temple than outside.

4 Wanting to become a Buddhist nun

'Do not touch, do not taste, do not handle' . . . These things
indeed have an appearance of wisdom in self-imposed religion,
false humility, and neglect of the body, but are of no value
against the indulgence of the flesh.
(Colossians 2: 21 and 23, NKJV)

In July 1983 I was drawn to go back to the international
forest monastery in the north-east of Thailand. This time I
wanted to stay for longer, to join the 'rains retreat', so that
I could live like a Buddhist nun without actually being one.
This three-month retreat is undertaken by Buddhist monks
and nuns every year from July to October (the rainy season).
They vow to stay in the temple, quietly developing meditation
and other Buddhist practices, and do not travel unless
absolutely necessary (traditionally because it was difficult to
travel during the monsoon season).

So I found myself back on the night train from Bangkok
to Ubon Ratchatani, then on the bus ride out into the
countryside. When I arrived there were no women staying
at the temple, and I would be the only woman there for most
of the three months. Everyone staying at the temple lived

separately in simple little Thai-style wooden huts on stilts scattered around the forest, with the nuns' and women's section separate from that of the monks. The living conditions were basic and I slept on a mat on the floor. We had no electricity and there were lots of mosquitoes which only increased with the rain. There were many dangerous snakes in the forest too, including cobras, which could spit harmful poison.

Our lives were simple and contemplative. Our main focus was meditation, which we practised on our own in our little huts or together, generally in the shrine room. There were various forms, including one called 'the practice of mindfulness'. The aim of this was to develop awareness and reach a state of detachment from the world by aiming to let all things go (whether physical or mental phenomena, such as thoughts, feelings, emotions). Buddha saw these things as impermanent and 'void of self', and believed that attachment to the world meant suffering. He thought this meditation helped to find the way out of that suffering.

Looking back, I see a great paradox here, in that the Buddha taught us to use our own efforts (we were to 'be a refuge unto ourselves only') to try to realize that we don't have a self. I now see that this is nonsensical, because we *do* have a self, we *are* here! A person cannot 'let go' of themselves or 'let go' of the world through observation and awareness. I no longer believe that the mind has the ability to let go in this way, nor was it ever designed to do so.

Other forms of meditation included contemplating death, and another was the practice of 'beaming out' thoughts of loving kindness to all 'sentient' beings in the universe. We had chants for these subjects too. The monks would talk of the 'benevolent universe' as if there was a great big Duracell battery of benevolence out there somewhere radiating loving kindness, but they never really explained what it was. I don't think they knew.

Our routine was fairly regular: waking bell at 3am; meditation and chanting (in Pali or English) from 4.30 until 6am in the main shrine room (this included all the monks, novices and interested lay people staying in the temple). The monks would then go out on the alms round, begging for food in the local villages. There were chores for me, sometimes helping in the kitchen to prepare supplementary food that had been offered to the temple for the one meal of the day. We then ate together, sitting silently in straight rows, in hierarchical order (with the monks and male novices first), in the shrine room. Then there was often a mid-morning nap after the heavy one meal of the day!

We all did various chores in the afternoon. I would sweep the paths of leaves, or clean the kitchen. The monks might mend the buildings and dwelling huts when necessary, or sew robes. Sometimes we would learn various Buddhist chants, usually alone in our little huts, then have an afternoon drink together, usually at the abbot's hut. In the evening there would be meditation, chanting and sometimes a talk from a senior monk (usually in English). Then I would go back to my little hut, walking through the forest in the dark, trying not to think about snakes, but looking out for them with lantern in hand.

The only day that differed from this was *wan pra* – the 'monks' day' each week which followed the lunar calendar, when we would rest more in the day and meditate longer into the night.

Our lives were really very simple – there was no telephone or other means of communication with the outside world, except through letters; no television, no music or dancing. I remember experiencing a lot of loneliness at that time; I had hours of isolation. Sometimes local Thai women came to visit me, but most of them could not speak English and I couldn't speak Thai or their particular dialect. However, they were very friendly and their smiles, encouragement and kindness were of great comfort to me.

There were many challenges and adjustments to living in such a different environment. Thailand was relatively new to me. There was much to learn about living in a temple too, such as how to relate appropriately to the monks and the local people. At times I felt a long way from home and I missed my friends.

I really looked forward to receiving letters. At the end of that year I was still at the temple, and my mum sent me one of her delicious homemade traditional Christmas puddings. It cost a fortune to mail as it was so heavy, laden with goodies like sultanas, raisins, nuts and brandy, but she didn't mind. She was determined that I wouldn't miss out. I was happy to share it with people at the temple.

Even though at times it was hard for me to be there, I was young and determined, and had enough encouragement to keep persevering with Buddhism and life in the temple. At that time there was nothing else that I would rather be doing. I felt I was in the right place.

The meal was one of the most exciting and interesting events of the day (certainly the one with the most sensory stimulation). Our food consisted of locally grown produce and a staple of delicious sticky rice that we would roll into a ball roughly the size of a small grapefruit and eat with our fingers. We ate chicken grilled over charcoal; curries of various kinds; *som tum* (spicy papaya salad); *dtom yum* (spicy soup); vegetables such as bitter gourds, carrots and *pak boong* (a green leafy vegetable that grows in water); fruits such as papaya, pineapple and custard apples; sometimes delicious Thai sweets made of coconut milk and many other delicacies. From the beginning I loved Thai food (except for the frogs and dung beetles that were occasionally included). We would have all our nourishment for the day in this one big meal eaten from a single bowl, for which I sat cross-legged on the floor near the back of the shrine room.

I learned to really appreciate the local Thai village people who supported the temple. Many of them were rice farmers, and they seemed to be some of the kindest and most generous people I had ever met, even though they were very poor. The women would usually wear sarongs, most of which they had woven themselves on looms in the village. The cloth was beautiful. Some of the villagers, both men and women, had black teeth and orange lips, which I found very strange at first, until I learned that this came from chewing beetle nut (from a native tree). Beetle nut, I've heard, is a slight stimulant, but I suppose it's the local equivalent of chewing gum – albeit with rather remarkable effects! I was never brave enough to try it.

One VSO volunteer who came to visit at that time told me that 80% of the children in the area were malnourished. Yet many of the families would give their best food to us each day, as they believed that by doing so they were 'making merit' (good karma) and would get a better birth in the next life. This belief has a powerful hold on Thai Buddhists and really affects their behaviour. The desire to 'make merit' is great, so much so that some are willing to experience great hardship in the present in order to do it.

Buddha incorporated the idea of karma and rebirth from Hinduism into his own teaching. ('Karma' here means volitional actions, done with intent, whether good or bad.) He believed that the effects of such actions continue to manifest themselves in a life after death, by being born again into one of the various planes of existence. 'Good' deeds would get you into a more favourable 'rebirth', while 'bad' deeds would get you into a less favourable one. Buddha also had his own definition of what good and bad deeds were.

As Buddha taught that there was no soul that went from one life (or reincarnation) to another, but only the karma of a previous existence, he didn't speak of a 'person', but of a 'being' going from one life to another. For example, a 'being' may be born a man in one life, a hungry ghost in the next, and then maybe an animal (perhaps a bear, goat or dog) after that, depending on what they had done in their former life. That's why in Thailand they treat dogs very respectfully, and many Buddhists would not even kill a rabid dog, as it could be the 'rebirth' of somebody's relative, perhaps a mother or mother-in-law!

Buddha's spiritual goal was to make no more karma, so that all and any becoming would cease.

This belief in karma, I have since learned, is in stark contrast to what the Bible says, for example in Hebrews 9:27: 'People are destined to die once, and after that to face judgment.'

At this point, however, I hadn't really thought much about life after death for myself, but I was looking for answers and this seemed like a pretty reasonable theory at the time, even though it was a bit bizarre in places. As I was impressed with other aspects of Buddha's teaching, I was prepared to take this on board too.

I met some Buddhist millionaires who were very generous to the monks, nuns and temples, as they had been taught that these things were 'high merit targets' and that they were able to earn a lot of merit for the next life by being good to them. They acted according to these beliefs, hoping at least to be born into prosperity again. Often in the poorer villages in Thailand, the temples are the most affluent places and the monks the most well-fed people. This desire to make offerings to the temple was reinforced by the monks' teachings, which the villagers would frequently come in to hear, particularly on the *wan pra* (monks' day).

The shrine room had a big Buddha statue in it, to which we bowed to on the floor three times whenever we entered or left the room. This one was a Thai image, about seven feet high and a golden-bronze colour. People living in a Buddhist monastery have to show respect to a Buddha image as part of their lifestyle. They also have to be respectful to the senior monks or nuns, bowing three times to them too as a sign of respect.

To one side of this shrine was a pickled baby in a jar and in a glass case nearby there was the skeleton of a village woman who had shot herself. These peculiar items had been offered to the monks by the villagers, to be used as objects of meditation – to help us reflect on death and impermanence. The women were asked to sit near the skeleton for the meditation times, morning and evening, and I didn't object, because at the time I felt that it was a useful object of meditation for me too.

I often sat there alone, looking at these completely lifeless remains of humanity. Sometimes at night it would feel eerie with the flickering candles as the only source of light, but this was life in the temple and I didn't really question it. If feelings of fear came up, I was taught to watch them come and go, not to attach to them, as was the case with all feelings whatever they were, and to contemplate the Buddha's teaching that there was 'no-one' having the feelings anyway.

Now when I look back, this scenario fills me with a deep sadness. It is such a picture of aloneness, darkness, death, bleakness and emptiness. It seems strange to me now, but then it felt quite normal.

Local funerals were held in the temple. Contemplating death and chanting about it is part of a Buddhist monastic's lifestyle, and the monks and nuns were involved in presiding over these ceremonies. I would know when a funeral was about to be held, not because I was told usually, but because the village people would start to bring wood for the funeral pyre. No sophisticated crematorium here. During the funeral, the body would be placed in a simple open coffin and the monks and nuns would go up the steps and look down on it. I remember I didn't want to do this the first couple of times, but eventually I felt I should press through and do it. So at the next funeral I asked one of the lay women staying in the temple if I could hold her hand to increase my courage, and I walked with her up the steps of the funeral pyre to take a look. Thankfully this body was a peaceful-looking one. I survived. This was the first of many dead bodies that I would see and 'meditate on' during my time as a Buddhist.

After being in the temple for some weeks, I decided that I wanted to shave my head for the first time. A shaven head in Buddhism is seen as a sign of renunciation, simplicity and giving up of vanity. From a practical point of view it is certainly cooler in a hot climate. The funny thing is, though, contrary to its intent and purpose, you can actually become quite vain about your bald head; it reveals your head shape and bone structure much more intensely and you can't help but notice who has the most striking features! It seems that we can't cut or shave our inherent beauty away.

I had already had my hair cut especially short before arriving at the temple and being surrounded by people with shaven heads made it quite easy to shave mine. It seemed more normal than having hair! Buddhist monks and nuns shave their heads at least once a month, just before the full moon. I asked one of the lay men, a kind Swiss man staying in the temple who was experienced in shaving heads, to do it for me and he agreed. As he began I felt a bit strange, realizing that I had never seen myself without hair before. At the end I was afraid to look in the mirror, so I just took a quick peek, looking at half of me first, then realizing that it was all right to look at the whole of me. I felt OK with what I saw. Another step had been taken.

The next morning, walking to the shrine room, I felt quite different. In my long sarong, simple white blouse and shaven head, I felt quite nun-like. Some village people in the temple grounds who saw me greeted me respectfully with a *wai* (Thai greeting, with hands pressed together), as if they thought I was a nun, and this pleased me.

Increasingly I gave most of my worldly possessions away, dressed simply and lived a life very similar to that of a nun. I spent most of the day alone, apart from meals, afternoon teatime and meditation times. I was always relieved and happy when another woman came to stay as it meant I had someone to talk to. It wasn't appropriate for me to spend much time with the monks or men. Occasionally the abbot would talk to me to see how I was doing, and I valued my time with him.

One night I was allowed to go and stay in the Thai nuns' section at the nearby temple. The next day an American missionary to Thailand called Hope Taylor came to the temple. It was her practice to visit the Thai nuns and foreign women, hoping for an opportunity to tell them about Jesus. Two foreign nuns, an American and a German, had come to know Jesus through Hope on one of her visits a few years before, and it was still the talk of the temple! She was a petite lady, Thai-size really, kind, extremely clear about her faith in God and full of the desire to share that faith with others. She devoted her life to telling and teaching others about Jesus, sharing the good news about him all over Thailand, whether travelling on the bus or in a taxi, or at a market, and some came to faith through her.

She arrived at my hut that day, uninvited and un-announced, and sat with me. (I later learned that she would pray and talk to the women as she felt God lead her.) So there she suddenly was, sitting with me in my little wooden hut. I remember her steely blue eyes, so blue, so concentrated, looking directly and penetratingly into mine as she repeated many times that 'Jesus is the only way, Jesus is the only way'. When she left, I was in a state of confusion for three days afterwards: her words had really caused me to think. I told the monks about her visit, but after a few days I returned to 'normal' and got on with my Buddhist life once more. Little did I know that many years later we would meet up again and I would become close friends with Hope.

After three months of being in the temple the rains retreat was over, but I wanted to stay longer as I still wasn't resolved about what my next step should be. So I asked permission from the abbot to extend my time there, and this was granted. One day, after I had been in the temple for nearly six months, I was walking up and down along the meditation path next to my little wooden hut when the thought came, 'Yes, I want to ordain.' And that was it: I knew then that I had to become a Buddhist nun.

We were ones who had 'given up the world', aiming to become detached from it. This finally seemed to be the answer I was looking for. I had gone from self-indulgence at one end of the spectrum to self-denial at the other, and it felt good. Giving up the world seemed a small price to pay for the promises of spiritual liberation and truth that Buddha appeared to be offering me. I trusted that his promises were right and that leading this sort of life would take me to the truth for which I was searching so deeply. With this hope I decided to ordain.

I felt that if I ordained in Thailand I probably wouldn't last long. The nuns had few rights there and they lived a difficult life, very much in the shadow of the monks and sometimes living more like beggars, which wasn't appealing to me. So I wrote a letter from Thailand to the American abbot in England, asking if I could join their community. He had worked hard to try and give the nuns better opportunities, and from the beginning I had felt that if I were to ordain, then I would want to be under his leadership. My heart immediately went there.

So I left my life of isolation in the forest. I had spent six months there. I said goodbye to the monks and my friends from the village, and some of them gave me gifts of hand-woven cloth for my mum. It was hard for them to give me presents, as I was giving most of my possessions away. I packed my few remaining things and was soon on the night train to Bangkok, then on the plane heading for England. From thinking, 'Would it ever be possible that I could be like them?' I was about to try to join them. What would it be like? Would they accept me? I was soon to find out.

5 'Narrow, boring Christians'

'Enter through the narrow gate . . . small is the gate and narrow
the road that leads to life.'
(Matthew 7:13–14)

I went to live in the Buddhist monastery in the south of
England in January 1984 and was ordained as a novice nun
within ten days of arriving there. The abbot knew I was keen
and dedicated, having spent six months in the forest temple
in Thailand. He had received news of me from the abbot there,
and so went ahead quite quickly with the ordination. He
didn't need to test my commitment. It was a cold February
evening when I donned the Buddhist novice's white robe and
'went forth', as they call it, becoming an eight-precept nun.
I was twenty-seven years old. The abbot led my ordination
in front of the order of monks and nuns, and I was the only
one ordained that evening. It felt right to be making this
commitment.

I chanted in Pali, taking refuge in the Buddha, his teaching
and the Sangha (the order of monks and nuns, the 'holy
ones'), agreeing to the following eight precepts:

to abstain from intentionally killing any living being;
to abstain from stealing;
to abstain from sexual relationships;
to abstain from lying, false, abusive or malicious speech;
to abstain from intoxicating drinks or drugs;
to abstain from eating after noon;
to abstain from dancing, singing, wearing ornaments,
    perfumes, going to shows;
to abstain from over-indulgence in sleep.

The abbot would choose names for the monks and nuns he ordained and he gave me a new Pali name that evening. I liked the meaning – it meant 'noble and good' – and from now on in the community I was known by this name (preceded by 'Sister'). It felt good to have a new Buddhist name. It represented the fact that I had taken another step in leaving the old behind, in 'detaching' from who I used to be and identifying more fully now with the ordained life. (Looking back now, I don't want to record or even remember this Buddhist name.)

My parents hated this new name and refused to call me by it. For them there was no way my name was going to change. My official name under law and according to my passport was still the same: Esther Louise Baker. They began to visit me quite regularly, not because they liked coming, but because they were concerned for me.

The nuns lived in a little cottage down the road from the main temple, which was a renovated Victorian country house. We also had a forest that had been given to us, near the cottage, and small huts and garden sheds had been built in there where the monks and nuns would sometimes live or go on solitary retreat.

The schedule was slightly different from that in Thailand – there we got up earlier as it was so hot during the day – but the essence of the lifestyle was the same. On most days, apart from the 'monks' day' once a week, we would have morning bell at 4am; meditation and chanting at 5am; chores at 6.30am; gruel and tea at 7.15am; work at 8.15am; the meal at 11.30am; work or receiving guests in the afternoons; drinks at 5pm; and chanting and meditation at 7.30pm. As I was only a novice, I was still free to drive a car, own a bank account and use money, which the monks and nuns could not.

On the full moon and the new moon, we would have a day off and try to meditate sitting and walking through the night, with a drink at midnight. Fortnightly, at the full and new moons, the fully ordained monks and nuns would recite all of their rules in Pali (for the monks all 227 of them!) before the evening meditation sitting.

I had ordained in the prime of life, as it were, at the age of twenty-seven, and some people ask me, 'Didn't you ever want to get married?' From the age of twenty-one, I started to be very much focused on the spiritual search which took priority over everything, including relationships and a career. Also, from childhood I had never particularly had a dream to marry or have children, not like some girls. And, although they said they were very happy, my parents' married life did not ignite within me a desire to settle down and marry. Being celibate was my preferred option.

The robe and shaven head of a Buddhist monk or nun are designed to reduce the differences and emphasis in gender. Accentuating male or female features is considered unnecessary for one who has 'given up the world'. It is not desirable as a celibate to attract attention for marriage or sexual purposes. Sometimes people who didn't know us had problems telling which of us were men or women!

I had a strong faith in Buddhism and was willing to do the things the abbot asked of us, as I really trusted him. I think I would even have cut off my right arm if he had asked me to (thankfully he didn't).

The monks and small community of nuns with whom I lived – most of them Westerners and a few Asians – were very sincere. They were seeking truth too and were willing to go through tremendous self-sacrifice to find it. I think that Westerners are drawn to Buddhism for all kinds of reasons. A high and lofty philosophy that doesn't include God can be particularly attractive to intellectuals. Although some were tolerant of Christianity, many of the people I knew had issues with God or the church, for one reason or another – as I had. Some had parents who had forced Christianity on them when they were children or teenagers. Some had been put off by seeing hypocrisy in the church. For others the idea of God just seemed ridiculous. I felt very at home with the way many of them viewed Christianity.

Several of the monks and nuns were very intelligent people and many had studied at university. Some had also lived self-indulgent lives – sometimes mixed up in sex, drugs and rock'n'roll. Then, becoming unfulfilled, damaged and confused, they went to the other extreme of giving it all up, seeking answers in self-denial and abstinence, looking for a way out of the suffering that their self-indulgent lifestyles had caused them. Several of the senior monks were American Vietnam veterans who had gone to Thailand for rest and recuperation during the Vietnam War and found refuge in Buddhism. It's a very subtle and sophisticated philosophy for those who want to lead a 'good' life, but have no personal experience of who God is.

One Easter time something happened out of the blue that struck me as quite unusual. I hadn't been a novice for long. It was Good Friday, and suddenly, for the first time in my life, I really wanted to know what had happened to Jesus that day. It wasn't rational; I can't explain why I suddenly wanted to know. I'd never been interested before. I asked one of the senior nuns, who told me in a very matter-of-fact way that it was the day Jesus had been crucified. Then on Easter eve

I asked again, and again on Easter Sunday, and I was told that this was the day that Jesus had risen from the dead. I still didn't understand what these things meant, but I was curious to know.

During this same Easter time, I was sitting alone in my bedroom at the nuns' cottage, in front of a little table on which I had made a shrine containing an image of the Buddha. I was looking at the shrine and then, in the silence, I turned around: there on the white wall behind me was a shadow of a cross. Sunlight had hit the window frame in such a way that it had reflected a perfect cross onto the wall. I stared at it, transfixed for a while. I wasn't thinking about anything in particular, just absorbed by the cross and its mystery.

After Easter had passed, my usual disinterest in and dislike for Christianity returned. In retrospect, though, I see that this strange occurrence was actually one of the preparations for things to come. God was starting to break through.

As a novice, my main role was to serve the community of monks and nuns, shopping and cooking for them, taking care of them and driving when necessary – a bit like being a servant to the community. I found my niche in taking care of the grounds too, planting trees and gardening in the various temples. My horticultural training had found a place to be used, at least in part. The grounds were large at two of the temples, so there was lots of scope with which to work, and the senior monks and nuns were grateful for my help. Buddhist monasticism is very hierarchical – the longer you have been ordained, the 'higher' the position you have in the community. For example, for more formal occasions such as the meal or meditation times, the more 'senior' person gets offered the food first, or sits in front of you in the seating order for meditation. So the novitiate is very much a testing time to see the extent of your commitment to the Buddha's teaching and to the community.

From time to time the monks and nuns would attend or conduct funerals and sometimes dying people came to live at the temple to end their days with us. When they died, we would usually keep the body in the shrine room and meditate on it until the funeral. We sometimes had elderly nuns living with us too. I often found comfort in being with them and enjoyed being part of the team taking care of them.

I was a novice for two and a half years, and over that time one compelling desire grew in me, which was to take the ordination of a full ten-precept nun. I really enjoyed listening to our abbot's teaching. Sometimes I would feel as if I was physically getting bigger as he taught. At times it felt like spiritual nectar to me.

Finally, after what seemed like a long wait, I took the higher ordination in the summer of 1986, alongside two other female novices. We were ordained according to age, and I was in the middle. One of them, whose head I had shaved when she first joined our temple, was to become a close friend in the community. Quite a few people came to watch, including my brother Derek and two of my close friends. My parents couldn't bear the thought and stayed away.

I took a personal vow to live as a ten-precept nun for at least five years. It was easy for me to take this, as I couldn't imagine that I would ever want to do anything else. Some monastics took a lifetime vow, but I didn't feel ready for that yet and thought I'd start with something a bit less grand. It felt good finally to be a ten-precept nun and I was excited to have got this far.

I now wore a long dark-brown robe, shaved my head and eyebrows at least every month and had a proper clay alms bowl, not the metal one of the novice. These small details in life took on a much larger significance for us as we had such few possessions and limited input from the outside world. I was now able to go on alms rounds in the mornings like the monks. I had become an official 'alms mendicant', a professional beggar. My food would be placed into my bowl each day and that would be how I would live, in dependence on others. It was now an offence for me to ask for food directly, but people could offer me food and put it into my bowl as long as it was before noon. Some Buddhists – English and Asian – would move house to come and live close to the various temples, so sometimes we would go on alms rounds and visit their houses when they invited us.

As we went about our daily lives and came into contact with other people, we weren't allowed to share openly about the Buddhist faith without an invitation – but we would sometimes attract attention by our appearance. With our shaven heads and long, baggy robes, we must have looked very strange walking down an English high street! When people were interested to know more about us, we could then share about Buddhism.

Sometimes we would have interfaith meetings at the Buddhist temple, when the abbot would invite Christian monastics and people from other faiths to attend. We would have discussions and debates and spend time together. I had taken my dislike of and lack of respect for Christians into the monastery with me. I continued to feel that they were narrow and boring. Claiming that Jesus is the only way to the Father seemed far too exclusive and limited for me. I couldn't make sense of that at all. At times I would try to convince some of the visiting Christians that God and nirvana (the Buddhist goal of emptiness) were the same. I really enjoyed sharing rather forcefully in this way with some Greek Orthodox nuns who visited us. They seemed particularly holy and devoted to Jesus and I tried hard to convince them. They would sit somewhat quietly and anxiously, almost as if they were holding their breath, waiting and longing for me to finish. They seemed relieved when I did and keen to leave!

I could see in some Christians' eyes that they started to doubt as I spoke like this: 'Are nirvana and God the same?'

I could tell that they weren't sure of their faith. Other Christians, however, had something in their eyes that was certain, something that could not be moved, shaken or negotiated with. I didn't know what it was. It was unfamiliar. I knew there was no point in discussing the matter further with these people, and left them alone.

In my eyes I had now gone up a rank. Things were improving: I was a junior nun, no longer a novice trying endlessly to keep white robes clean. The practice of meditation and mindfulness was our main work and I was even more committed than ever to living like this.

As monastics we served the wider Buddhist community. We would receive food and other offerings; chant for them at a wedding blessing or funeral; receive guests; offer teaching and guidance; and try to incorporate all of those aspects as part of the practice of mindfulness. The higher ordination meant I had more rules to follow and had to take more care in my conduct and daily life. It meant a deeper commitment to the teaching and monastic code of the Buddha – and possible humiliating punishments, like having to walk at the end of the line when collecting food at the mealtime, if I were to slip up and break the rules.

I could now not be alone with a man, and even with the nuns or other women we were encouraged not to hug or express feelings or emotions very much, so we became used to a lack of physical contact with people. Buddha taught that feelings and emotions could lead to attachments, which he said were the cause of suffering and bondage to this world. Instead we were to watch feelings come and go, and not to identify with them. Denying my humanity and living this way made sense to me, and so I was willing to do it. When Siddhattha's son was born, he called the child 'a fetter', demonstrating how central to his teaching was the idea of detachment from family life.

All this was unknown to my parents, who continued to visit me faithfully and regularly. They were even more concerned after I had taken this higher ordination, fearing that I had become more helpless, weak and lost.

Soon after my novitiate, some of us moved to a newly acquired monastery, an old school on top of a windy hill near a large town to the north of London. This, like the former monastery, was a mixed community of monks and nuns. We lived separately, but certain activities we would do communally, like eating meals, chanting and meditation. There was a strict code of discipline between the monks and nuns, although naturally attractions did sometimes arise, once resulting in a senior monk and a nun disrobing to get married.

After ordination I eventually started to teach Buddhism and meditation, and could give advice to some of those coming to the temple looking for help. I was also able to encourage and help women seeking ordination. Highlights for me at the time were teaching at the Buddhist Society in London and taking the Buddhist funeral of a man in Essex whom I had met. I finally felt as if I was getting somewhere!

Visiting Christians would sometimes share their views and try to tell me about Jesus, but their words were like water off a duck's back. They simply couldn't find a place to 'land' in my mind or thinking. I was irritated by them. 'God, God, where is this God they keep talking about? Where is he? Why are they so narrow-minded, always insisting that Jesus is the only way? What can they see that I can't?' My attitude was to try to convince them that what we believed was all the same, then maybe they would shut up and leave me in peace. I was generally glad when they left.

These antagonistic feelings were reinforced by some of the talks we heard in the monastic community. One senior monk in particular would often say disparaging things about Christianity. He said how gory and violent the symbol of the cross was, with a bloodied, dying Jesus, and compared this to the peace of a Buddha image. How I could relate to the talks of this senior monk at that time, and how I enjoyed his reflections! How pathetic and insignificant this Jesus seemed to me! 'OK,' I thought, 'at best, maybe Jesus was a good and wise man, but as to the other claims about being God, it seems ridiculous to me.'

In no way could I possibly imagine that before long, this 'sad' and bloodied Jesus was to enter my life in the most dramatic, life-changing way. He would completely drain away my sure and long-standing Buddhist faith: like the lifeblood that runs out of a slaughtered calf after it has been cut with the knife, my certainty in Buddhism would drip away, drop by drop, until it was lifeless. It was drained away so that something much greater could be given. The unimaginable and unthinkable, for me, was about to happen.

6 Parents' heartache

'The child's mother grabs the sharp end of the knife.'
(South African proverb)

While Buddhism was fascinating to me, for my parents, particularly my mother, my ordination was very hard to accept. They simply couldn't understand it and from the beginning had a deep mistrust of Buddhism. It was far too alien. My mum, dad and brother came to meet me at the airport when I flew back from Thailand, just before I ordained as a novice. I was wearing a long black skirt and had a shaven head. For some reason I hadn't forewarned them of my great change in appearance.

As I approached them, Mum had to ask my brother if that was me, as she couldn't recognize me. She didn't know her own daughter; I was too unfamiliar. She turned away in shock and disbelief, sobbing as she realized. What had happened to me?

I stayed with the three of them for the weekend, but it was my brother who took me to the monastery, which I wanted to get to quite soon. My parents couldn't face it. When it came to the time of my ordination, my mum was absolutely devastated about me becoming a Buddhist nun. She feared I was being brainwashed. However, much as they hated it, they visited quite regularly, usually about once a month, simply out of concern for me. Mum in particular wanted to bring me things that she thought I might need: she hated the thought of me being hungry or cold, as she was beginning, in her thinking, to be aware of the 'deprived' kind of life I was leading.

The first time Mum saw me receiving food in an alms bowl as a novice, it was unbearable for her. She simply couldn't look at me and wept, heartbroken. All of our food, whatever it was, such as curries, meat, potatoes, or pudding, was all dumped into the same bowl as a way of denying ourselves some of the pleasures of the world. Mum was horrified. What was I doing? What had driven me to this? My mum loved to cook and always presented food beautifully, but now she had a daughter living like a beggar, silently sitting on the floor eating with a little spoon and her hands!

The temple was about seventy miles from their home, and when they were coming to visit, Mum would spend the previous afternoon baking lots of cakes. Often I would give her cakes to the whole community, as it was our custom to share things offered to us, but some 'allowable' things she insisted that I keep for myself!

Mum genuinely couldn't see any good thing in Buddhism. Why did I have to give up a night of sleep every week? Why did I have to eat gruel from a mug, line up for my food, not sleep on a proper bed? She thought it was simply wicked to work so hard with no evening meal or proper breakfast. One day, when she was visiting, she told the abbot some of this, hoping he would change things – at least give us a meal in the evening – but that wasn't to be. She felt increasingly helpless. There was little she could do to make me see what she saw. I was so engulfed by it.

At one point I was hopeful that my parents were beginning to accept and understand my lifestyle. They had been on holiday and bought me a small Chinese Buddha image from a market stall. (As I owned practically nothing, it was hard to buy me presents.) They knew this would mean a lot to me, and I was delighted and touched by their thoughtfulness.

On one occasion, I was out with Mum in a supermarket, my head freshly shaven. It wasn't fashionable at that time, and the girl at the till was rather alarmed by the way I looked. She said sarcastically, 'Now *this* is the haircut I want!' My mother felt that she could fall into a hole, she was so embarrassed. As for me, when people reacted like this, I just took it as material for meditation. If people were delighted or shocked at what they saw, it didn't make that much difference to me.

After that Mum asked me not to walk with her in public. That must have been very difficult for her. She explained that it wasn't that she didn't love me, but she felt that if anyone asked her why I was doing what I was, or why I looked so strange, she simply didn't have an answer – it was all too heartbreaking and weird for her. She is a lady who loves to dress well, taking pride in herself, and she felt ashamed and bewildered by me being in a robe. I complied with my mum's request, knowing that it was important to her, but it hurt that we were poles apart in understanding each other. I had no idea just how heartbreaking all of this truly was for her.

At one point we were incredibly cold, having moved into a new temple, and there wasn't enough money for sufficient heating. We were told to deal with the cold as a practice of renunciation, tolerating the hardship of it with barely any heating for two quite bad English winters. This had long-term effects on my health and for a long time afterwards made me very sensitive and averse to the cold.

Mum always said how ill and thin many of the monastics looked – so much suffering and self-denial for what? I couldn't see what she meant. We all looked OK to me. As the years progressed, my parents became increasingly worried about my physical and mental welfare. It was a hard lifestyle. I didn't realize it, but gradually, over a period of years, these practices – eating little, sleeping little, intensive meditation and sensory deprivation – began to take a great toll on me.

Once, by chance, after I had been living for many years in the temple, Mum happened to catch a glimpse of me in the shower. She was alarmed to see me looking so thin. She said I reminded her of someone from a concentration camp. I hadn't done well on one meal a day for nearly eight years. My metabolism is much more suited to eating little and often. I understand now that Mum was worried that if I didn't leave soon, she would lose me. She was probably right.

At that time, I was blind to it. I couldn't see the effects this lifestyle was having on me. It was true, though: I had become very thin and tired and was struggling increasingly with minor health ailments. In my mind the hardships seemed a small price to pay for 'ultimate truth'. Quietly, to myself, I continued to dismiss my parents for not understanding.

'If ever you leave this monastery, you'll have to take a course in being normal again!' my father said to me at one point. Sometimes it was hard for him even to have a simple conversation with me, because I was so out of touch with the world. He was shocked that I couldn't remember when the football season was, despite our family home being near a football ground. By now I had spent many years trying to 'let go' of the things of the world, and in this instance it had worked!

I do remember that sometimes, when we found a newspaper, even an old one, we read it with relish. Deep inside there was a hunger to know what was going on around us. Our hearts were hungry, even though our heads said these things were empty and didn't matter.

My mother tells me that on their journeys back home from the monastery they were always very quiet, unable to talk. They felt completely helpless and sad. What could they do?

They didn't have any answers, they didn't know what to do. And so they continued with what they had been doing. Mum would start again to collect and prepare the gifts that she felt would be helpful for me for the next time, for yet another heartbreaking visit.

In retrospect, their generosity and determination to see me – even their helplessness – was truly my parents' love for me, and I am so grateful for it now. All of this did very much help to sustain me through my time there. I can see that now. I was so 'spellbound' with it all and so determined to press on, that Mum and Dad never dreamed that I would leave. No-one anticipated the enormous change that was about to come. But my mother's heartache regarding this was soon to be over.

7 Doubting Buddhism

What a wonderful and mysterious power truth is. How it sits
atop the most resistant head and darts into the darkest heart.
That head and heart may not choose to act on the truth or to
acknowledge it. The person may even repress it very deeply, but
once truth is spoken, there is a place in the human heart that
knows it has heard truth, and it will have to wrestle with it from
then on. It is the truth, and Truth Himself, who changes people,
structures and nations.
(Leanne Payne[1])

I had never really doubted Buddhism, and was often impatient
with other nuns who did doubt or wanted to mix in other
types of Buddhism with 'our' Thai Theravada Buddhism. 'Why
do you need anything else,' I would ask impatiently, 'when
we already have everything we need in this teaching?'

Then several of the Buddhist monks and nuns from the
monastery attended an interfaith meeting at Canterbury
Cathedral. This was an incident that affected me powerfully.
I remember walking happily along the road to the cathedral
with other monks and nuns from our nearby accommodation.
I was looking forward to the meeting. I didn't expect to see

Christians with banners, shouting and protesting at the fact that we were going into the cathedral. There was a long line of them, waving banners in our faces, implying strongly that we had no place going into the house of God. They weren't nasty or aggressive, but seemed firm in their belief and opposition to us. I couldn't understand what had upset them and it actually made me think a lot. It was a key moment in me questioning my Buddhist faith. I remember feeling quite down and depressed all weekend about it. I was very quiet and subdued, and spent as much time alone in my room as I could.

I had looked forward to this meeting, and now I couldn't enter into it at all. I didn't feel angry, upset or offended that the Christians had opposed us going into the cathedral – but I was mystified. What was it that they were so opposed to? What did they know that I didn't? I was truly puzzled. I thought that I had found the truth and understood God, but when I looked into their eyes I saw hostility and it made me question. Just when I thought I had it all worked out! In my mind I had concluded that God and nirvana were the same, but perhaps I didn't really know him; perhaps they weren't the same. Some years later I was very grateful to those protesters, as they had provoked me to question and had sown seeds of doubt.

Not long after that meeting, something strange started to happen to me. I started to want to go and sit in churches and be with Christians. If Christian monks or nuns came to the temple, I would seek their company. I no longer wanted to antagonize them, but just wanted to be there with them: there was something comforting and attractive to me in their presence. My head denied God, but my heart was beginning to warm to his people.

I had made a new friend, too, in the village, since we had moved to the temple north of London. She was an Anglican nun called Sister Elizabeth who would come and visit us sometimes. She was quite elderly and occasionally needed help. At times I did little odd jobs for her around her tiny cottage. Sometimes, I remember, she would come and ask me to cut her hair and it always felt like a great privilege when she took her wimple (head covering) off so that I could cut it. I enjoyed spending time with her and liked it when she came to the temple. Occasionally I would go and visit her in her cottage and we would drink tea, eat biscuits and chat together. I didn't know at the time that she had started to pray for me.

I had been ordained in total for about six and a half years and was back at our original monastery for a while in southern England. It was usual to receive visitors, lay men and women, staying with us in the various monasteries. At this time we had a drug addict lady staying with us and I really wanted for us to be able to help her. (I often found myself spending time with the more fringe-type people who would come to the temple seeking answers.) But I could see that there was nothing within Buddhism that could really set this lady free. We had high ideals, but that wasn't enough. Too often now I had discovered that we couldn't really help such needy people. I realized that not even I had truly been set free and healed at a deep level.

This woman talked with great enthusiasm about a video she had seen of Jackie Pullinger, an English Christian lady who worked with drug addicts and the poor in Hong Kong. She said that through the power of prayer these drug addicts were being miraculously released from their addictions. She told me how much she wished that would happen to her.

I started to question Buddhism in earnest. Sometimes I would look at the senior monks and nuns and think privately that they were not all that wise or liberated after all, despite all those years of meditation and 'giving up the world'.

One night around that time, we were having one of our all-night meditation sessions to observe the full moon. We would usually start at about 7.30pm with chanting and a talk by a senior monk or nun, and then we would meditate, walking or sitting, through the night until about 4 or 5am. The only break was for a drink and some medicinal substances at midnight. We had a younger American abbot who would occasionally let us watch a 'suitable' video to help us stay awake. Sometimes in the middle of the night, as we were meditating, we would hear a crashing sound: even a senior monk could have fallen over, fast asleep, much to the amusement of some of us. So watching a video would help to avoid such an embarrassment and keep everyone awake, at least for a while!

As it happened, this particular night we were going to watch the same video the drug addict lady had told me about not long before, called *The Law of Love*.[2] The younger American abbot was open-minded about other religions – some Buddhist monastics are. (I wonder now whether such people are open to other religions, as they are still looking for ultimate truth.)

We watched this video at midnight, and the effect on me was tremendous. Jackie Pullinger and her helpers would pray in the name of Jesus and by the power of the Holy Spirit, and drug addicts would be freed from their addictions, often completely painlessly. For the first time in my life I could see that there is a living God – not a lifeless philosophy, but a living Person, real, powerful, true and personal. I now knew that he is our Father and Creator and I knew that I could no longer deny his existence. I saw miracles of the destitute being healed, not only physically, but also spiritually. I saw this with my own eyes and from that moment something inside me changed. It was not possible for me to deny it.

The people in the film had a certainty about the spiritual life I was seeking; a fullness and meaning that I knew I didn't have. I had given up everything for it, but I had not yet found it. They had such freedom and life. It made me feel spiritually destitute in comparison. I couldn't explain what it was they had, but I knew I wanted it. It was a simple, childlike desire that arose within me. Amazingly, in a room of thirty people – monks, nuns and visitors – it seemed that only I had been deeply touched in this way.

The following morning I was devastated. I felt ill, really physically weak and confused. I walked up to the temple from the nuns' cottage for gruel, feeling shattered and arriving late, only to hear the abbot say, 'Well, that was a real waste of time watching the video last night.' I was in pieces inside, but stayed silent. I did confide in one nun, in my weakened state, about how watching the video made me feel so spiritually poor. She agreed with me, but it hadn't really impacted her life in any significant way. I somehow felt 'undone' inside. Something deep and foundational within me had been disturbed, touched, awakened. It was beyond my control and confounded my understanding. I felt a real mess and very debilitated.

Not long afterwards, I secretly asked my mother to buy me copies of Jackie Pullinger's two books, *Crack in the Wall* and *Chasing the Dragon*.[3] My father went to the Christian bookshop to get them for me and they brought them on their next visit. I kept reading and rereading these books and started to become even more confused. Sometimes I was afraid to look too much at them, as I feared that if I did, I would become a Christian! This was very threatening. Had I become institutionalized as a Buddhist? I had lived in a temple for so long. What would it mean if my life were to change? It was a bit like having been married to someone for a long time – the whole Buddhist thinking and lifestyle of a nun was so much part of me.

I knew that my Buddhist faith was being really challenged. I had never seriously doubted Buddhism before and I didn't like it; I liked to be sure. I kept the reading of these books to myself, even though some of the monks and nuns were interested in other faiths so it wouldn't have shocked them.

I didn't want to announce how strong my interest in them was, nor how deeply the video had affected me.

To doubt like this somehow felt very inconvenient, just when I was starting to climb up the monastic hierarchy. I tried to push the whole thing away. I said to myself, 'I'll not take any more interest in Christianity. It makes me feel too confused. I've never doubted and I'm not going to start now.' I put Jackie's books at the back of my cupboard with quite some determination and immersed myself again in Buddhist life. I tried to 'let go' of any thoughts or interest in Christianity. Enough was enough! I did not want to be bothered by it any more.

But it wasn't as easy as that. We used to have long meditation retreats in the winter, for two or three months each year, when we would stop all activities in the monastery, not accept any guests and simply meditate. This year during the retreat, I felt really fearful at times. I tried everything (from a Buddhist perspective) to try to calm myself, but it didn't work.

One sleepless night, in desperation, I called out to God. I just said a quick little prayer from my heart: 'God, if you are real, please come.' And God came! After I had prayed I felt a sense of peace and well-being flooding my heart and body. The fear was gone. It had lifted and within minutes I was fast asleep. It was absolutely amazing. This was the first time I had invited God to touch my own life, invited him in and asked for his help – and he had come. I knew he had answered my prayer; the feelings of peace, contentment and well-being continued, which was remarkable compared to how I had been feeling before.

In a way, things got worse for me, now that I knew for myself that God was real. I had seen that he was real in others through the video, but now I knew it for myself. I was even more confused, as intellectually I was still denying that God existed. I had been affirmed in this view by following the Buddha's path and I agreed with it in my head – but my heart and my spirit now knew that God was real. This tension within me started to feel unbearable at times, like two sides pulling hard in opposite directions, vying for my attention and consent, stirring up incredible confusion and spinning in my mind. Never in my life had I known anything like this.

I wanted to be in church. I wanted to be baptized and to pray. Having been so uninterested in Christianity for decades, I honestly didn't know what those things meant, or where those thoughts and desires came from. No-one had taught or told me to want those things, but I knew that was what I wanted to do. What was happening to me? Was I cracking up, after years of monasticism. Was I simply no longer able to cope with the endless rules and restrictions? Or had I really come to know God?

I knew almost nothing about Christianity. I had read very little of the Bible and there were very few Christians around to whom I could talk. However, one day my senior nun asked me to talk about Buddhism to a Christian group in the local town. (The nuns were not aware of the deep turmoil inside me. I felt I couldn't share it with them.) I was delighted. 'Finally,' I thought, 'I can talk to some Christians.' Even better, I was sent alone, so I would have more freedom to ask them what I wanted. They were a lovely group of young adults wanting to find out more about Buddhism and monastic life. I made it clear from the beginning that I would tell them about Buddhism if they would *please* answer my questions about Christianity.

It was a good evening for me. The young people helped me a lot and one of the women sensed my hunger to understand more about Christianity. Not long afterwards, she bravely came to the temple with a Bible for me. She didn't realize what she had done – my own Bible! I read it and read it, and the more I read it, the more confused I became. Jackie Pullinger's books came back out from the cupboard again, and when I felt confused I would open *Crack in the Wall*. It contains lovely pictures of Jackie, her helpers and the street sleepers in Hong Kong. Looking at them, I would become peaceful, clear and inwardly strengthened again. In the end, taking central place on the Buddhist shrine in my room was *Crack in the Wall*, open at a picture of Jackie praying for a street sleeper, with her words written beside the picture: 'What is important is that we be like Jesus, loving someone even if he seems hopeless. We are going to try whatever happens, that is the heart of Christ.'

Truly this was a crisis of faith.

8 Choosing life

'[When] you return to the LORD your God and obey His voice,
according to all that I command you today . . . with all your heart
and with all your soul . . . the LORD your God will bring you back
from captivity, and have compassion on you . . . therefore choose
life, that you . . . may live; that you may love the LORD your God,
that you may obey His voice, and that you may cling to Him, for
He is your life and the length of your days.'
(Deuteronomy 30:2–3, 19–20 NKJV)

Sister Elizabeth, the Anglican nun from the village, came to
visit me one day at the monastery, and brought a friend with
her. Alison Metcalfe was a Christian and she lived near my
home town. It was the first time she had entered a Buddhist
temple. I later discovered that she had felt quite intimidated
by the large statue of Buddha that she saw at the entrance,
but it didn't put her off.

She told me enthusiastically about her faith and church,
Christ Church. She invited me to go there with her if I got
the opportunity. I liked Alison and wanted to keep in touch
with her. She had been an Anglican nun and so at some level
I could relate to her, even though the foundations of our two

faiths were different. Once or twice I telephoned her from the temple for advice and looked for an opportunity to go to church with her. I wasn't aware of it, but after our meeting, she too started to pray for me daily while walking her Scottie dog up and down the muddy fields where she lived.

In May 1991 I visited my home town, staying with my mother and father, along with a senior nun and a novice. This was my chance. The senior nun didn't want to go to church (it was the same nun who had answered my questions about Easter a few years before), so she stayed at my home, but the novice and I went with Alison to Christ Church. It was Pentecost Sunday – not that I knew what that meant – and the vicar gave a talk and an elderly man led a time of prayer afterwards. People were praying and singing in a similar way to how I had seen Jackie Pullinger and the team in Hong Kong pray on the video, so I felt a sense of familiarity being there.

Not long before this, I'd had a dream that I was in a boat with two elderly men who were Christians, and I really wanted them to pray for me. The man who was leading the prayer time at Christ Church came over, looked right at me and said some things that encouraged and comforted me. I was instantly reminded of the two men in the boat in my dream.

Afterwards I spoke to the vicar, Revd Will Whitehouse. His eyes were steady and sure; here was a man whom I knew was certain of his faith. I was glad to talk with him, even though it was brief. He had been told in advance by Alison that two Buddhist nuns would be coming to the evening service and had felt a little anxious about our visit. However, the Lord had pointed him towards a Bible verse from Jeremiah 1:8, 'Do not be afraid of their faces' (NKJV).

It is interesting for me now to hear the first impressions that these people had of me. When Revd Whitehouse first saw us, me in a brown robe and the novice in white, he was taken aback by our completely shaven heads. He felt that from the outside he had no way of knowing whether we were male or female. He also noticed how pale and undernourished we both looked. Leading worship that night was Clare Marks, a faithful Christian and one of the church's leadership team. Unlike the vicar, she didn't know that we were planning to attend. She tells me that she had been struck by how very thin and gaunt I was, and noted a blank look on my face. She sensed my discomfort as I stood motionless looking at the music band, a bit like a lost soul waiting to be told what to do. She felt in her heart, 'Praise the Lord that they have come.' It must have been quite an event for this church community to have us at their Sunday evening service!

After I was back at the temple again, I found myself wanting to be a Christian more and more. I wanted to worship God, but I was so trained in the Buddhist meditation techniques of detachment that when these thoughts arose I would try to 'let them go'. Thankfully, they could not be dismissed so easily and persisted.

My doubts about Buddhism intensified. I started to keep a journal, which I realize now is an excellent thing to do in a spiritual crisis. I had one section for Buddhism and one for Christianity, and I wrote down my thoughts and doubts, the advantages and disadvantages for each, as they became clear (even if they were contrary to each other on different days), to try to weigh up what it was that I was really feeling and believing.

I started to feel repulsed at bowing down to the Buddha image, and thought how empty and pointless it was bowing to the senior monks and nuns. I had done these things in earnest for years and now they seemed really meaningless.

The abbot's talks also became intolerable to me. I had so loved to hear him speak, but suddenly I couldn't bear it any more. I would smuggle earplugs into the talks to blot out his words. It's not easy subtly to put in earplugs when you are all sitting cross-legged in straight rows, motionless on the floor – but I rammed them in hard and hoped they wouldn't fall out, and that no-one else would notice them and ask what the problem was!

Looking back, I understand that this was God working in me, draining out the 'lifeblood' of my previously strong Buddhist faith. My faith was becoming completely bankrupt.

I began to realize that when some of the monks and nuns said they knew God, it wasn't really a true recognition of God. It was more of an eclectic type of understanding, thinking – as I had done for a long time – that nirvana and God are the same. I now knew this was not true. God is in no way recognized, acknowledged or worshipped in Buddhism. Buddha's teaching regarding God is very subtle and deceptive. He *did not deny* the existence of God, *nor did he acknowledge* the existence of God. However, although Buddha did not deny the existence of God, in everyday Buddhist practice God is neither acknowledged nor worshipped. In reality, there is no place for God at all in Buddhism. The foundation of Christianity is God, the foundation of Buddhism is not, so the two faiths are fundamentally different.

I remember hearing of a senior monk in Thailand joking with a group of monks from his temple: 'When you go to England, call Buddhism Christianity.' I realized now how inaccurate it was to confuse the two.

I started to refuse to teach Buddhism or meditation. The doubts were so deep in me that I didn't want to be responsible for deceiving others. I wanted to teach people to pray, but I didn't really know anything much about that yet myself.

I asked the senior nuns for some space, which they kindly granted. I was still living fully under the nuns' rules at this stage, but my heart was drifting out, like an old-fashioned ship sailing out of port. I kept waiting for it to turn back to its harbour, but it didn't. Some of the monks and nuns knew that I was struggling. Sometimes people went through periods of doubt, so they didn't pressure me. For this I was grateful.

I called my mum. I didn't tell her about the confusion I was in, but for the first time she heard doubt in my voice about being a Buddhist nun. She could tell I wasn't so happy to be at the temple. The tone of my voice was different. I understand that with some excitement she told my brother Derek that she thought I would be leaving. Wanting to protect her, he cautioned her not to get her hopes up.

It was like being on a pendulum at times, being swung up and down all over the place, even spun out of control. Truly it was horrible, a nightmare of *such* mental confusion. At times I tried to resist the obvious changes that were happening to me, and attempted to rationalize them. Maybe I just wasn't coping any more. Maybe I just needed to carry on as a nun with more determination than before. It seemed as if there was a battle in and over my mind. I hated being so unclear.

I found a prayer from the Greek Orthodox tradition that I liked very much: 'Lord Jesus Christ, Son of God, have mercy on me, a sinner.' I used this prayer during the meditation sessions (instead of meditating) and started to ask God for guidance. I was hungry now to learn how to pray and to pray directly to God; Buddhist meditation had become meaningless for me. I no longer wanted to 'let go', or to focus on emptiness and impermanence. I was hungry to reach out to God.

At this point my internal turmoil was at its height and something was about to break. It was in this state that I fled the monastery that momentous Sunday morning. Spontaneously taking the opportunity provided by the absence of most of the nuns and monks, I took to my heels and sped down the hill to the church. I was just composing myself while the last churchgoers made their exit. I had to find some peace. I had to talk to the vicar. My journey out of Buddhism was gathering speed.

I later found out that the vicar who prayed with me that morning was Revd Richard Mason. Amazingly, he had been completely unfazed by my seeking him out, later saying he had even been blessed by it. He knew I was in a spiritual crisis and realized how hard it would be for me if I did disrobe. For a start, I didn't own anything. I had no money and barely any material goods apart from the few possessions of a Buddhist nun. Also, Revd Mason and his wife were concerned as they didn't know if my Buddhist abbot would give me a hard time if I asked to leave. They were about to go on holiday at the end of that week and knew that they wouldn't be there to help me much after the coming Tuesday's appointment, so they called a friend of theirs, another local parish priest, Revd Cyril Ross, to tell him what had happened, in case I contacted him while they were away. They began to pray for me in earnest from that time on. Despite their concerns, they felt a peace that God would take good care of me.

A couple of days later, I went to my eagerly anticipated meeting at the vicarage. This time I left the temple with a novice, as it would have been improper to leave alone. We walked in the direction of the vicarage. I didn't want her to know where I was going, so I asked her to go on ahead and said that I would see her back at the temple. It was a sound plan; I didn't think she would suspect anything and she didn't. I snuck off towards the vicarage, where I was warmly welcomed and ushered into Revd Mason's study. We chatted and he read these verses of Scripture to me, spoken by Jesus in John's Gospel:

> 'Let not your heart be troubled; you believe in God, believe also in Me. In My Father's house are many mansions; if it were not so, I would have told you. I go to prepare a place for you. And if I go and prepare a place for you, I will come again and receive you to Myself; that where I am, there you may be also.' (John 14:1–4 NKJV)

No-one had ever spoken words of Scripture directly to me and for me before, and I was delighted and intrigued. I asked him, 'Does that mean I've become a Christian?' He replied, 'I believe the Lord has really touched you.' These were the words of confirmation I was waiting for. This man of God had confirmed for me that I had become a Christian, that all this spiritual confusion and unrest was because I had come to know God. With his few words, I now knew *for sure* that I had to disrobe. My mind became full of confusion when I tried to think about Buddhist things, but was full of peace when I thought about God, prayed to him or saw Christians, whether these were pictures in a book or direct meetings.

I called Mum to put her out of her misery. She couldn't believe it; she asked me twice if it was really true! She was absolutely delighted. Never in her wildest dreams had she dared to expect this. 'It's a miracle!' she said. I could hear the great relief and joy in her voice. She had always said that she didn't mind even if I became a street sweeper. For Mum, almost anything would be better than being a Buddhist nun. I tried to explain to her that God had touched me, that I had become a Christian now, but in Mum's mind I had left because of Jackie Pullinger, and if it wasn't for her I would never have come out of the temple. From the beginning she had full support for Jackie, who made a lot of sense to Mum, unlike Buddhism. She even started reading the book *Crack in the Wall* herself and telling people about it.

I realized that there were many broken areas within myself where I longed to receive healing, but through Buddhism and meditation they had been contained and suppressed rather than inwardly transformed. I had fought Christianity for a long time – as long as I was able to resist God and find what I was looking for in Buddhism. At the core, I hadn't wanted to change my way of life. Yet God had persisted with me, even in my denial of him, and now the only way to peace and truth was to surrender to God.

The nuns and monks had been my closest friends for seven and a half years, yet now I could no longer agree with them about Buddhism. When they talked about the Buddha's teachings I didn't argue, but just stood there quietly, unable to relate to it all any more. Generally they treated me with respect, even if it was hard for them to understand what was going on. No wonder it was puzzling and painful at times for some of them. Truly I had become like a stranger in the midst of the community in which I had lived for so long.

My mind became calmer and clearer. Thankfully, the turmoil of confusion had subsided and I was experiencing God's peace, which I found that Jesus had promised to his disciples:

> 'In Me you may have peace. In the world you will have tribulation; but be of good cheer, I have overcome the world.' (John 16:33 NKJV)

Understanding that I had come to know Jesus, even though I didn't really have words to describe what had happened to me, was like a door opening for me – the door of the monastery. I knew I had to walk through it and leave. We would soon be going into the rains retreat. There was no time to lose. I needed to ask to disrobe urgently, before I was committed for another three months.

9 Disrobing

Beware lest anyone cheat you through philosophy and empty
deceit, according to the tradition of men, according to the basic
principles of the world, and not according to Christ. For in
Him dwells all the fullness of the Godhead bodily; and you are
complete in Him, who is the head of all principality and power.
(Colossians 2:8–10 NKJV)

I started to tell a few of the nuns that I wanted to leave. One
of them was the nun with whom I had ordained. I knew she
would find it difficult, as we were very close and had confided
in each other much over the years. I tried to find the right
moment to tell her; I was aware that there was no easy way
to do this. In my own heart I was sure by then that I had to
leave – in a sense I had already gone. But how was I to break
it to someone with whom I had shared so much?

'If you disrobe, then change your mind and decide to come
back, you'll have to start from the beginning again.' She was
very concerned. She knew that I'd had a strong Buddhist faith
before and had respected me as a nun. It was hard for her to
comprehend and to trust that what I was doing was right.
My attitude had changed so much from how she had known

me to be for so many years. I tried to reassure her, but she remained puzzled.

Another nun with whom I had lived for much of the seven and a half years broke down and sobbed, saying, 'What has happened to you?' I tried to be sensitive as I told some of them that I had come to know God and that things had changed now. Some of the nuns could see this, even if they couldn't understand it. None of them mocked or intimidated me. I think some feared that I was taking a 'step back down' into the world again, perhaps back onto the slippery slope of worldly pleasure and indulgence.

I really couldn't explain clearly the changes in me. I didn't know much about God or Jesus, but in my heart and spirit I just knew that I had to be a Christian. Many things were pulling at me to stay, but the quest for truth which had been my main drive into Buddhism was stronger than my attachment to Buddhism itself. I no longer spoke the same language as the nuns and monks with whom I'd lived for many years. I no longer believed in the promises of the Buddha and I was no longer committed to his teaching.

I now knew that not all spiritual paths led to the ultimate truth. Buddhism had not taken me there. It had led me elsewhere, but not there. I thought to myself, 'If I was on my deathbed now, would I have done everything possible to find truth?' I realized that the answer was 'no' and that I must disrobe and become a Christian. In all my rebellion, sinfulness and idolatry, God had remained committed to me, and now he was calling me out and onwards into a life with him.

The next step was to ask the abbot for permission to leave. It was important to me to leave the community well. I could just have left at that moment, but I had lived with these people for a long time and wanted to disrobe in an appropriate way. I didn't want just to run off, as some had done in the past. When this had happened, their memory was not one that was respected by the monastic community. A bit like knitting, I needed to cast off the stitches properly, to leave well.

After seeing the vicar on the Tuesday, I asked to see my abbot. I had just completed the vow that I had taken at the time of ordination, to be a ten-precept nun for five years. The completion of this vow felt liberating to me: I had fulfilled my obligation and was no longer bound by it. I met with the abbot two days later, on Thursday 25 July. I was apprehensive about this meeting. I was going to ask to disrobe and I couldn't imagine that he was going to like it!

However, as I walked into the room, I felt the presence and peace of God with me. I knew I wasn't alone. I went onto my knees and bowed three times to the abbot to pay my respects, as was the custom when in the presence of a senior monk. I sat on the floor while he sat on his chair, and we talked. I felt that we had been very close during my seven and a half years in the temple and I had really respected and trusted him for most of that time. Eventually I told him that I wasn't exactly sure why, but I wanted to disrobe. I shared with him the picture I'd had of the ship sailing out of port and not coming back. I couldn't tell him directly that I had become a Christian, as I felt it wasn't appropriate. I knew that one of the senior nuns had told him, but we didn't discuss it. He looked at me and said, 'You have had a complete collapse of faith,' which was true. Actually, he helped me to understand what had happened to me. My Buddhist faith had gone, collapsed and was drained of life; no longer did I want to bow down to the image of a man, Buddha, when I could worship the Creator of the man, who was God. It seemed pointless.

With time, I started to see what I had been doing all of those years. I had been trapped in idolatry, which is to worship any *created* thing rather than the *Creator*. I had been devoted and had given my life to the subtle and sophisticated philosophy of a man, Buddha, a created thing, rather than worshipping the *Creator* of everything, who is God. I saw that having anything as a spiritual goal other than the One True God is idolatry: it felt meaningless and I couldn't bear to do that any more. How jealous God must feel, I realized, when he saw me worshipping or bowing the knee to something or someone he had created rather than to him! I later discovered the words in Deuteronomy 4:24 which say that God is a jealous God and felt that they were written for me! I now fervently wanted to worship and acknowledge the Creator (Father, Son and Holy Spirit, the Holy Trinity, Three in One) and not any thing that God has made.

From reading the Bible I saw that there are numerous references to idolatry and that it is something God really detests, understandably so. Its dangers are often mentioned. The words in 1 John 5:21 spoke out to me: 'Keep yourselves from idols.' And in Hosea too:

> What have I to do anymore with idols?
> I have heard and observed him.
> I [Father God] am like a green cypress tree;
> Your fruit is found in Me.
> Who is wise?
> Let him understand these things.
> Who is prudent?
> Let him know them.
> For the ways of the LORD are right;
> The righteous walk in them,
> But transgressors stumble in them.
> (Hosea 14:8–9 NKJV)

'If you have found something that is more helpful to you, I give you my blessing.' These words from the abbot were truly astounding – he was blessing me to leave! 'When would you like to disrobe?' he asked.

'As soon as possible,' I told him, 'as some of the nuns are finding it quite hard to deal with what has happened to me.'

'How about Sunday?' he said.

'Fine,' I agreed.

I was quietly amazed and grateful. He hadn't asked me to wait for a week or two to check if I was doubting, but was releasing me instantly. I felt that he knew I was sure. He asked me if I had any clothes to disrobe into, as by then I only had the ten possessions of a nun which included three robes, one alms bowl, a needle case and a razor, and no money. I said, 'No, but I'll find some.' We chatted a bit more and then I left, positively astounded and delighted that I was leaving so soon, and that he had blessed me to go. I couldn't believe it.

I then took a walk with my senior nun, through the field that was part of the temple, where I had planted many trees. I broke it to her that I wanted to disrobe and amazingly she too treated me with respect and didn't try to make me stay or question me unnecessarily. She also gave her blessing for me to go. It is hard to explain, but once I had decided to disrobe, I felt as if I had a ring of protection around me. I could feel the presence of God; I felt safe and protected by him in each situation, as if no-one or nothing could harm or touch me. I didn't feel any sadness or loss as I spoke to my abbot or senior nun and during all this time I didn't shed one tear. My sights were firmly set on the way out now.

I went into the store cupboard with the nun who looked after it. I had three days to get some clothes together before the disrobing ceremony with the abbot and senior nun. She gave me a few bits and pieces, including a green shirt. I wanted a skirt too, hopefully in a similar style to the nun's sarong, like a cylindrical skirt, that I had worn for seven and a half years. We never wore lay or ordinary clothes, so the thought of wearing something so different came as rather a shock: I had been in the Buddhist robe for all that time. She found a green skirt made from a curtain. 'That'll do,' I thought. It was the closest to what I was used to. My father had been right:

I would need to go on a course to become 'normal'. There was a huge amount of adjusting to do!

The length of time between first seeing the Jackie Pullinger video and disrobing was a period of about a year. I had fought hard against change, but in the end God came through. I have often questioned why I was the only one touched by God in this deep way when we watched the video together that night. Why me? Why was I the only one to come to know and experience that God is true, when there was a room full of monks and nuns who were all 'seekers' watching with me? The only answer I have to that is that it was God's grace for me – I had done nothing special to deserve it. For some reason, in his mercy he was gracious to me and touched me.

> Because of his great love for us, God, who is rich in mercy, made us alive with Christ even when we were dead in transgressions – it is by grace you have been saved . . . in order that in the coming ages he might show the incomparable riches of his grace, expressed in his kindness to us in Christ Jesus.
> (Ephesians 2:4–5, 7)

One nun put her finger on it exactly: 'You've come to know God, so there's no point in you being here any more.' Then she said, 'I'm jealous you've met with God.' I was really touched by her vulnerability and honesty. There was a sense that she knew she hadn't yet found what she was looking for, that there was something much more, much greater than she had.

It came to the morning of 28 July 1991, the official disrobing ceremony. It was a Sunday morning and I sat on the floor waiting for my senior nun to join me. I was sitting alone in my Buddhist robe with my alms bowl beside me, feeling peaceful and expectant at the thought of the liberation that was about to come. As I waited, I could hear the sound of church bells ringing out from the local village church.

It was as if they were gently calling for my attention. I lifted my head towards the sound of them, and focused on their comforting, soothing, sweet chimes. I began to smile to myself (perhaps there was a celebration going on in heaven!) and I could feel God's presence with me. He was with me. I felt calm, composed and content.

The senior nun came in and sat beside me, and we waited for the abbot to arrive and perform the disrobing ceremony. There would just be the three of us. Sometimes disrobing ceremonies were a bit grim.

The abbot came in and sat on his seat. We bowed towards him. I had brought a present for him – the plump, bronze, laughing Chinese Buddha that my parents had bought for me. I wanted to keep nothing Buddhist any more, whether books, Buddha images or anything else. This was a good chance to part with it. I looked at him, saying that I would like to give him this Buddha image, it had meant a lot to me and it reminded me of him (he was a large man too). The abbot burst into peals of laughter. This was not going to be one of those grim ceremonies: there was a lightness of heart, even from the abbot. We chanted the necessary chants, then I went out to change into my green shirt and the skirt made from a curtain. When I came back, I gave the abbot the Buddhist symbols of 'going forth': the robe and bowl.

The process went very smoothly. I did look rather peculiar in my new green suit, but I didn't mind. I had disrobed, and I knew I needed to be patient with myself in the adjusting process to come. I was now set free. Materially I had practically nothing – no money, no possessions and only a few clothes out of the store cupboard – but I had hope, I had God, and I felt rich. I trusted that God would take care of me. If I had been able to live as a Buddhist nun and 'professional beggar' for seven and a half years, how much more would our true and living God take care of me. Disrobing truly had been an act of trust and faith.

My feelings at that moment resonated with the apostle Paul talking about the joy of becoming a Christian after many years as a Pharisee. His words in Philippians echoed my own experience of coming out of the strict, legalistic life of Buddhist monasticism:

> But what things were gain to me, these I have counted loss for Christ. Yet indeed I also count all things loss for the excellence of the knowledge of Christ Jesus my Lord, for whom I have suffered the loss of all things, and count them as rubbish, that I may gain Christ and be found in Him, not having my own righteousness, which is from the law, but that which is through faith in Christ.
> (Philippians 3:7–9 NKJV)

For thirteen years Buddha's teaching had felt like a mountain of truth standing solidly behind me. When I came to know Christ, that mountain collapsed into a pile of dust and rubbish. For me the illusion had been exposed and I could see it as it truly was. What had felt so real was truly worthless and insubstantial.

I thank God that he rendered my life as a Buddhist nun meaningless and pointless. I had felt his presence so closely as he gave me the clarity and strength to leave. I couldn't have managed to leave in my own strength: I was too institutionalized, my mind was too bound up in the intellectually seductive teaching of the Buddha, and I was too attached to the tradition and position I was in. But God had provided a way. I was now ready to go fully into my Christian life, no longer an idolater worshipping the created, but rather a worshipper of the Creator of all things. A new beginning indeed. It felt wonderful.

10 Leaving the temple

'I am the LORD your God . . . You shall have no other gods before Me. You shall not make for yourself a carved image – any likeness of anything that is in heaven above, or that is in the earth beneath, or that is in the water under the earth; you shall not bow down to them nor serve them. For I, the LORD your God, am a jealous God.'
(Exodus 20:2–5 NKJV)

I had decided to spend three more weeks at the temple, which the monks and nuns agreed to allow. I had lived in a Buddhist temple for so long that I needed a little time to adjust to my new lifestyle. I didn't ever go again to meditation, or to hear any Buddhist teaching or talk, or to a ceremony. I just stayed there, preparing myself for the world outside.

After the disrobing, someone kindly gave me £10. This was the first time I had handled money in five years. I remember going to the local village shop, buying some crisps and eating them with great relish. I smiled all the way back to the temple: not only had I bought them myself, but I was eating solid, 'non-medicinal' food after noon, which I hadn't done for many years. I felt that each 'normal' thing I did, such as using money again, was a mini-conquest, another step towards acclimatizing to life outside the temple.

The following morning I went to visit the local Anglican vicar and his curate, who happened to be his wife: Cyril and Mary Ross. They led the church on the other side of the hill from Revd Richard Mason's church and were the couple whom Richard had called in case I needed to contact them while the Masons were away on holiday. I had heard of them anyway, as they were well respected locally.

I had called Mary a day or two before. I didn't know it, but they were having a church meeting at the vicarage at the time. I explained to Mary on the phone, 'I'm a Sister from the Buddhist temple and I want to become a Christian.' I didn't realize the stir and excitement that I caused! Usually they had little to do with the monks and nuns, but were aware of us in our distinctive garb as we walked about the village. They were about to become more intimately acquainted.

When I knocked on the vicarage door in my freshly disrobed state, Mary opened it. I still had very little hair and was dressed a bit strangely. She warmly welcomed me in, sat me down with a cup of tea, and I shared my story about having just disrobed. She and her husband Cyril were amazed and delighted and started to plan how to help me. From the beginning I warmed to them and enjoyed being with them.

Over the next three weeks, I took the short walk down the hill to their house several times. Dear Mary took time to teach me the basics of the Christian faith. She was aware that I had no real Christian background and knew little about the Bible. She was a wonderful mentor, keen to teach me: so clear, so wise and so passionate about Jesus. She soon taught me how to pray, which I had longed to do, and we spent time praying together. She lent me some worship music tapes, and I remember so enjoying listening to the worship from Taizé. One of the songs, 'Oh Lord hear my prayer, Oh Lord hear my prayer, when I call, answer me', resounded again and again in my mind.

I had so many questions, but I trusted that the understanding I needed would all come in due time. There was so much to learn in my new-found faith. I was very hungry to find out more and take it all in.

The most important thing for me was that I had discovered that God is real. In all his seeking and 'renunciation' of the world, in his desperate quest to find his way out of old age, sickness and death, Buddha had missed the most important truth of all: God.

I had come to know that the absolute truth for which I had been searching was God. He was it, and there is no other. Jesus' words began to be full of meaning for me: 'I am the way and the *truth* and the life' (John 14:6); 'You will know the *truth*, and the *truth* will set you free' (John 8:32). I realized that these were not empty words, but something that could really be experienced. I was beginning to understand that he came into this world to reveal to us that he is truth. Amazingly, God himself is the fulfilment of the longing and quest for truth and the real meaning of life: 'The Lord is the true God; He is the living God, and the everlasting King' (Jeremiah 10:10 NKJV).

Having not understood the Bible at all, I now devoured it avidly. I began to know deep in my heart and spirit that it is God's truth to us, full of his life, meaning and help, unchanging and non-negotiable. It started to become so alive and relevant to me. 'The grass withers, the flower fades, but the word of our God stands forever' (Isaiah 40:8 NKJV). Jesus said, 'Heaven and earth will pass away, but my words will by no means pass away' (Matthew 24:35 NKJV). Mary was helping to open up the Bible's riches to me.

During one of our times together we were seeking a place to talk and pray in the church, only to find that the cleaners were there, so we sat in the churchyard on a gravestone. Mary told me that as a Christian I was to let nothing or no-one come before God. Anything, even a job or a friend, could become an idol. She told me that if something or someone was becoming too important in my life, I was to 'give it to God'. Everything and everyone belongs to God. She told me that Buddha images are idols, the lifeless symbols of a man made of wood and stone (which I realized by then), but that the symbols in a church, for instance crosses and figures of Jesus, are all reminders and aids to take us to God and are not in themselves to be worshipped. I loved talking to Mary, and Mary felt in her turn that I was easy to talk to and eager to learn. She had no doubt at all that God was in this.

The thing I found hardest to accept was that I did not have to strive to earn salvation. In Buddhism I had been taught that spiritual development depended on my own effort. Buddha taught his disciples to be a refuge to themselves, and so I was tempted to try to do it all myself. Mary explained to me some of the mystery of the cross. She said that Jesus had done all that was necessary for my salvation through his death and resurrection. The price had been paid by him.

She told me to give to Jesus all the things I'd done wrong.

'It's not fair on him!' I protested.

'But that's why he died,' replied Mary.

'Really?' I said. 'Well, he can have it all. How do I give it to him?'

And she explained it very clearly.

All I had to do was believe in him. I could just accept God's free gift of grace and salvation. Before, as a Buddhist, I would have thought that sounded too easy, a bit pathetic really. Why did I need a saviour and someone to do it for me, when I could do it for myself? Now I realized that all my efforts, however hard or earnestly I tried, could never make me good enough. I had become righteous in God's eyes simply by having faith in Jesus and choosing to live in obedience to him. I had found a place of great rest.

I still had few possessions, very little money and not many clothes for normal living. Mary wanted to help me and so gave me some clothing, but I was much taller than her, so we went to the charity shop to buy a skirt.

This whole experience was such a learning curve for Mary too, she told me. She remembers how surprised she was to learn that in Buddhist monasticism very little physical contact is permitted, not even a handshake, let alone a hug or the kiss of peace. Being freshly out of the robe, I wasn't used to these normal signs of affection. She realized it must have been a difficult time of adjustment for me, coming into the real world. Being 'born again' had extra connotations for me!

At one time before I disrobed, I wondered how I would continue to live a morally pure life without the multitude of rules under which I had been living as a Buddhist monastic. Would I suddenly start to collapse morally without the 'scaffolding' of law to uphold me and rein me in? The answer was here: by Jesus living in me. As I look to him and keep my eyes on him, by his grace he will give me the strength and power to live well. I found this summed up beautifully in Colossians 1:27: 'Christ in you, the hope of glory.' The teaching of Jesus is for the life he puts in us, not for our own right-eousness, which can never be enough, but his. There is now a greater One living in me, whose name is Jesus.

The insights of Christian writer Oswald Chambers gave me such a helpful, clear perspective on understanding purity: 'The real deep crisis of abandonment is reached internally, not externally. The giving up of external things may be an indication of being in total bondage.'[1] He helped me to see that as I deliberately committed my will to God and main-tained our relationship, living in obedience to him, that is how I would be able to live in moral purity. The external giving up of things, which I had done for so long, paradoxically easily becomes a deep form of bondage.

When I disrobed, I didn't in any way feel less than a nun or inferior. Jesus was now my holiness, wisdom, sanctification and redemption. I was set free to enjoy the godly aspects of his world. It was no longer against the 'rules' to sing, dance, wear cosmetics, dress in other clothes than robes, go to the cinema, drive a car, use money, eat after noon, or wave my arms around in public! These rules seemed utterly like bondage to me now; I was enjoying freedom in Christ – not freedom to sin, but freedom to truly live and embrace life.

One day, after talking to her husband, Mary suggested to me that it would be good for me to have a little ceremony in their church one Sunday, soon, before I returned home to my parents, to affirm my faith in Christ. I had 'cast off the stitches' of Buddhism now and it would be good to declare my allegiance to Christ consciously and publicly, especially after thirteen years caught up in Buddhism. I thought this was a wonderful idea.

Not long after that, therefore, I took part in a simple ceremony at the church, to reaffirm my commitment to Christ, witnessed by the local congregation. Mary and Cyril had prepared it specially (with the blessing of the area bishop), and it took place on 11 August 1991, led by them. This was rich and full of deep meaning for me. It was so good to declare my faith before others; now it wasn't just me and a few others who knew about it, but a whole congregation. It was a clear sign that I was putting my past life as a Buddhist behind, and was now able to go forward in Christ.

After the three weeks were up, on 17 August 1991, my mum and dad came to collect me from the temple to take me home with them. We popped in to have a farewell tea with Richard and Anne Mason at the vicarage on our way back. It was good to see them before I left. Finally I was going, and it felt great. My parents were thrilled. My father, who was seventy-five years old by then, never imagined that he would see me out of the Buddhist robe in his lifetime.

Looking back, I so thank God for dear Revd Richard Mason and his wife Anne, and Revds Mary and Cyril Ross. All of them really were God's messengers sent to help me in a time of great need and vulnerability. I will always remain extremely grateful to them and I still keep in touch with them all.

What a paradox! I had travelled so far, in terms of distance, lifestyle and spiritual searching, looking for truth – and yet now my parents were taking me home and I would be attending a church literally just a few miles away from where I grew up. What I had been looking for in all that searching was never far away from my own back door!

11 Starting a new life

'I have come that they may have life, and have it to the full.'
(John 10:10)

Back in my home town, I had felt so at home at Christ Church on my first visit as a nun that I never questioned which church I should join. So I started going there immediately and am still a member to this day. Revd Will Whitehouse and his wife Rosemary gave me a very warm welcome. They are both marvellous Bible-believing Christians and the teaching they provided laid a great foundation for what was to follow.

Life outside the temple started with me living with my parents. In the beginning I wasn't able to work. I would be up for a few hours and then have to rest. I was quite shocked at how weak I was physically. A gradual debilitation had crept in almost unnoticed by me, but now I was able to see it. I took the first few months to rest and eat a lot. From being painfully thin, soon I was gaining weight and slowly getting stronger.

It felt so good to be able at last to meet with Christians regularly and to be in church. I was warmly embraced by the body of believers at Christ Church: they were very kind and thoughtful in so many ways. Some invited me round for lunch or took me out for tea, befriended me, or invited me to interesting conferences and seminars. They were really like a spiritual family taking care of me. Many of them couldn't quite believe the transformation from what they'd seen on the previous Pentecost Sunday, and some of them still talk about it.

Some found it hard to relate to the situation from which I had come. In fact, I could see by their reactions, the distance their jaws dropped when I told them what I used to do, that it was not an insignificant thing to have been set free of Buddhist monasticism. Gradually it started to dawn on me just how amazing it was to have got out.

Will and Rosemary knew I needed to continue to become familiar with the basics of the Christian life and the Word of God. They seemed to know just what I needed at the right time. I trusted them and looked to them for guidance. I was thrilled when they offered to send me to a part-time Bible study course being held by a local community church. This was not just academic learning, but very much practically based with an emphasis on the outworking into daily life of what was being learned. I had limited funds, but Will and Rosemary offered to meet this need so that I could get a good grounding in the faith early on in my Christian life. I was really inspired by their repeated kindness and thoughtfulness towards me.

Being people who themselves were deeply prayerful, they emphasized the importance of developing a prayer life. They taught me practical steps on how to speak and listen to God, how to know the difference between God's voice and my own imaginings, and how to receive pictures and scriptures from God. We would do this together in prayer groups. It was amazing to watch God speak to us through various members in the group, using each one in a different way to communicate with us – a corporate communal time with God which was so different from the solitary meditation that I'd done for years. Many of the church members developed the foundation of our understanding of prayer through these times.

Buddhist meditation is not at all like Christian prayer and cannot in any way be likened to it. Christian prayer has God firmly at the foundation of it. The relationship between God and the believer is central; he relates to us and we relate to him. The foundation of Buddhism is not God.

I remember talking to Will, saying that having given my life to Buddhism for so long, I was keen to serve Christ and hoped that within a year of being a Christian I would be on the mission field. He was very wise and cautioned me to be patient. Of course, he was right. In fact, not long after that, God told me clearly that I wouldn't be going anywhere for three years. At that point I really relaxed into life in my home town and church, knowing that it was a preparation time and that it was OK to spend it just building myself up in the faith and readjusting to life outside the temple. I felt impulsive, but God wasn't in a hurry.

At first, living with my parents, I found their world was almost unbearably noisy (though probably quite normal compared to other people), with the telephone ringing, the television and radio on, and loud voices. I hadn't appreciated what a quiet world I had been living in for so long. Rather insensitively, I would tell them how noisy they were! When I went to the cinema for the first time in nine or so years, I was struck by so much sensory input. It was nearly too much: big screen, huge people, loud noises. My mind and imagination were full of these pictures long after I left the cinema, and I realized I had to be very careful what I looked at. Sensory deprivation had made me very sensitive. It doesn't have this effect on everyone, but I knew I had to be careful. I remember the first time I went swimming after disrobing:

it took great courage as I felt 'naked' in my costume, having been fully covered from my ankles to my neck and wrists for many years.

After resting for over four months, living at home with my parents, I began to work as a live-in assistant to an elderly lady not far from church. I was used to looking after older nuns in the temple, so this was familiar to me and I enjoyed it.

Will announced in church that they would be starting a mission fund as the church leadership believed that before long God would be sending missionaries out from Christ Church. I was so excited to hear this and keen to support it. In my heart I thought how much I would like to be a missionary sent out by Christ Church. Little did I realize that I would be the second missionary to be sent out.

One night, about six months after I had become a Christian, I woke up at 3am and sat bolt upright in bed. I was acutely aware of all the wrong things I had done in my life – in other words, my sin. I suddenly thought, 'I've got all this sin that has never been confessed: sexual sin, idolatry, the occult, sins of my family.' I hadn't consciously been thinking about these things, but now felt deeply convicted that I had to deal with them. I knew I needed to talk to Will. When I did, he explained that this was the Holy Spirit working in me to cleanse me, as it is our sin that separates us from God. He advised me to take some time to pray that the Lord would help me remember all that I needed to confess, and then write those things out on paper in categories. A week or two later, clutching my list, I met up with Rosemary and Clare Marks to start to confess.

Even after years of Buddhist practice and confessing any violation of the rules under which we lived, nothing in Buddhism had ever truly freed or cleansed me from my sins, or even given me a true definition of what sin is. (Only the Creator of the universe can truly define sin; a person's understanding alone will not be enough to define it accurately.) That's why the memory of them had come back. Sins can be contained and suppressed through meditation, but they are not finally dealt with by it. As Buddha was only a man and long since dead, there was nowhere for my sin and brokenness to go. There simply isn't a place of spiritual authority or power within Buddhism sufficient to deal with a person's sin. I now knew, however, that Jesus, as perfect God and perfect Man, had risen again three days after his death. By his rising he overcame the power of sin, death and hell, so sin has a place to end in Jesus, as he has overcome it. There is no other place to be found where sin ends except in Jesus. The great news I had discovered was that anyone can now come into an intimate relationship with God because of what Jesus has done on the cross.

So, as humbling and difficult as it was, I confessed all the various sins that the Holy Spirit brought to my mind, and was finally washed clean of them. I came out feeling like a different woman – I felt so clean inside, and a new way of life was set before me. This was such a good beginning and foundation to my Christian life, and I have been grateful for it ever since. I would encourage all new Christians to go through this process, to confess and repent of their sin early on. It can help avoid feelings of unworthiness and a sense that you are living under the condemnation of past sin. The practice of the confession of sin is now integrated into my Christian life. I consider it a very important part of my ongoing Christian walk.

Will and Rosemary suggested also that I consciously and deliberately renounce Buddhism by name, along with all the idols and past occult activity in which I had been involved, asking Jesus to break the ties and bondages that I had with those things. This I was happy to do. Jesus has the power to set us free from the influence of anything that is an idol or not pleasing to God. His is the name above all names. They explained the two kingdoms that are described in the Bible – the kingdom of God and the kingdom of darkness. Jesus makes this clear when he says, 'Whoever is not with me is against me' (Matthew 12:30).

I understood that we are either with him or against him, and that there is no third neutral place where the two kingdoms live happily together. As a new Christian I was reassured to learn that 'he has rescued us from the dominion of darkness and brought us into the kingdom of the Son he loves, in whom we have redemption, the forgiveness of sins' (Colossians 1:13).

I had rejected God since childhood and had been involved in some occult activities in my younger days. I now saw that these things had prepared me for coming to Buddhism. It's interesting that many Buddhists – Western and Asian – easily get involved in other forms of idol worship, spirit worship, animism, the occult, fortune telling, ancestor worship, etc., as they all sit happily together in the same kingdom. One thing that Buddhism doesn't sit well with is Christianity!

Understanding about the different kingdoms also helped to explain the tremendous spiritual battle I had been through before disrobing, the real war over my mind that had made it so hard for me to come out of Buddhism. As a Buddhist I had thought I was on the path of truth, but I wasn't. I had been leading a 'good' life, but unbeknown to me I was caught up in idolatry and deception. As a person wearing the Buddhist robe I appeared 'holy' and 'good', but spiritually I had been trapped in darkness. When God's Holy Spirit touched me, I came alive in a new way and then the battle began. I had come to know God and was alive in my spirit, but the bondage over my mind and thinking from Buddhism was trying to keep me away from him. That was why I had been so very confused and felt torn in two directions when I was a nun. The enemy of God distorts truth and goes to great lengths to mimic and masquerade as truth with the aim of deceiving many – a master of disguises whose true nature when revealed is nothing but an illusion, bent on destruction.

As Rosemary Whitehouse prayed, she asked the Lord to forgive me and told the powers of darkness to go in the name of Jesus and through the power of his shed blood. Rosemary had a clear impression in her mind of several black demons like pathetic tattered bats cowering for a moment near the fireplace in her sitting room, where we prayed, and then disappearing. She was reminded of the verses in Isaiah 14:12, 16–17:

> How you have fallen from heaven,
> morning star, son of the dawn . . .
> Those who see you stare at you,
> they ponder your fate:
> 'Is this the man who shook the earth
> and made kingdoms tremble . . .
> and would not let his captives go home?'

Rosemary felt that because of my verbal confession and repentance to God, they had to let go of their grip and go without fuss (see pp. 145–148 for useful prayers for this purpose).

At the end of all the sessions, Will came in and prayed that all of us in the prayer group would forget the sins that I had confessed, which was a great relief to me!

Confessing was hard. I thought, 'How can I let these good Christian women know what I have done in my past? It's so shameful!' But it's amazing that Jesus truly did die to wash our sins away and to break the power of shame. After I had confessed to him with these ladies as witnesses, my sins lost the power to come back and accuse me. I had never felt truly clean in Buddhism, but finally I felt like a newborn babe deep inside my soul and spirit.

I was helped so much by the wisdom of Will and Rosemary. I see the great importance and need of mature mentors and leaders in the worldwide church, people ready to guide, challenge and teach us. Without such help we remain weak and immature. I thank God that from the beginning I had great teachers who were always willing to encourage, disciple and support me.

I knew that I could take three years to be prepared, but what then? What was I being prepared for? That was soon to become clear.

12 A new door opens

Brothers and sisters, think of what you were when you were called. Not many of you were wise by human standards; not many were influential; not many were of noble birth. But God chose the foolish things of the world to shame the wise; God chose the weak things of the world to shame the strong . . . It is because of him that you are in Christ Jesus, who has become for us wisdom from God – that is, our righteousness, holiness and redemption. Therefore, as it is written: 'Let those who boast boast in the Lord.' (1 Corinthians 1:26–27, 30–31)

I remember that on one of my first Sundays at Christ Church after disrobing, Revd Will and Rosemary Whitehouse invited me to Sunday lunch. It was a lovely opportunity to get to know my vicar and his wife better. They were fascinated to know how I had come to Christ. After I explained, immediately Will and Rosemary said, 'We know Jackie Pullinger – she visited Christ Church a few years back.' In fact, Rosemary had first met her in London through a mutual friend who had been at school with her.

I was amazed. I had thanked God so much for the way he had used Jackie in my life, but I wasn't sure if I would ever meet her. After they had listened to my story, Will said to me very clearly in an uncompromising tone, 'You *must* write to Jackie and tell her what happened to you. It will be such an encouragement to her and the brothers and sisters in Hong Kong.' He promptly handed me her address. (The brothers and sisters are the community of helpers and those being ministered to who are with Jackie.) I knew I had no choice and it was actually such a buzz to be able to write to her. By this time I had been disrobed for a mere five weeks.

Within a short time I received a letter back. Jackie thanked me for writing and said how touched she had been by my letter – so much so that she had read some of it out for her people to hear. She wanted them to know that because of their faithfulness and testimony, the Lord had touched me and released his healing power, even while I was in a Buddhist temple. She was delighted, too, that Will and Rosemary were taking care of me and that I was in such good hands. She also said that if possible she would like to meet me. I was thrilled!

As it turned out, a few months later Jackie told me that she would be going to Westminster Chapel in London, the church of the well-known American pastor R. T. Kendall, on Sunday 23 February 1992. Could I make it there? I arranged to travel to London with a dear friend called Hannah. Hannah had lived in Hong Kong and knew Jackie, so this was a great support for me.

When we got to the church it was packed with several hundred people. Jackie was there with four Chinese brothers and one of their wives whom she had brought with her from Hong Kong. She told us that between them the brothers had been on heroin for over seventy years and had been in prison over forty times (most had been Triads, Chinese gang members). I kept looking at them. It was amazing. They all had that 'fullness of life' that had touched me in the video.

My heart welled up with gratitude, as I thought, 'These are the ones who have shown me Jesus!'

Jackie spoke in power of God's heart and love for the poor, and of how God has chosen the lowly and despised ones of the world as they cannot boast in anything except Jesus. As they receive Jesus, there is nothing else to see in them except him. God has chosen the poor to be rich in faith. You could hear a pin drop; it was as if her words were fuelled with the authority of God, commanding our attention. I was drinking this in. On so many levels I felt like one of those poor ones with nothing else but Jesus.

At the end of the meeting, there was an extended time of prayer, including an invitation for people to accept Jesus as their Lord and Saviour. Then Jackie said, 'I feel there are some people here who aren't sure that they have eternal life. You can be sure.' I had read this in the Gospel of John: 'For God so loved the world that He gave His only begotten Son, that whoever believes in Him should not perish but have everlasting life' (John 3:16 NKJV).

I felt puzzled. I was certain that I believed in Jesus, but did I know that I would spend eternity with God, after life on earth had ended? I realized that I wasn't sure about this, so I went forward for prayer, even though it felt a bit embarrassing. I didn't want to miss out on any steps towards deeper understanding, and a kind lady prayed for me.

I started to realize that to be a Christian means that I will have a relationship with God and be with him *for ever*. In fact, this is the very reason why I – and everyone else – had been created: to come into an intimate, godly relationship with our Almighty Creator and Father through Jesus, which continues after this life has ended. We will be in his marvellous, holy presence eternally. Life with him after passing from this world will be gloriously different from our life on earth. 'He will wipe every tear from their eyes. There will be no more death or mourning or crying or pain, for the old order of things has passed away' (Revelation 21:4).

What an amazing hope that is, promised to me and to all who would receive Jesus! Truly life without God *is* ultimately meaningless and empty. There is no real sense to it without him, and it seems that many people get stuck at this point, even intrigued by it, as I had been for so long. Buddha found this emptiness and made it his goal, but this is *not* the end of the story. I had found that God himself is the source and fulfilment of all being, becoming and meaning. God made each person in his image and so each one of us has inestimable value. He created, creates and sustains life. I and all things he created do exist (to claim that 'no-one' is here and all things are empty, as Buddha did, is simply not true). And God has a perfect purpose and meaning for his creation. For it is only in him that we 'live and move and have our being' (Acts 17:28): outside him we don't. When in his mercy God enabled me to realize that, I was able to move on and see beyond emptiness as my goal. I could celebrate and embrace the true purpose of life, no longer needing to deny or empty it of its source and meaning.

At the end of the meeting Hannah and I had our chance to meet Jackie. It felt as if God had mysteriously brought us together and when we finally did meet, although it was for the first time, it was like seeing an old friend. From the beginning I just loved being around the brothers and sisters from Hong Kong. Some of them prayed for me to be able to speak in a special prayer language called 'tongues'. Wonderfully I received it, as they prayed. It has become a great help in my prayer life. I was so incredibly blessed by this first meeting with them all.

Back at home, I heard that Jackie had suggested to Will, my vicar, that I should have a full immersion baptism. Will agreed and it took place one Sunday evening in front of the congregation, in the small baptismal pool inside the church. My mum and dad came along too. Two of us were being baptized that evening: me and a man who had formerly been a Jehovah's Witness. It felt good to be alongside him, a suitable companion! As part of the baptism liturgy there is a series of questions and responses between the vicar and the candidates. I found these to be a very helpful confirmation of my new-found faith.

Do you turn to Christ?
I turn to Christ.
Do you repent of your sins?
I repent of my sins.
Do you renounce evil?
I renounce evil.

Do you believe and trust in God the Father
 who made the world?
I believe and trust in him.
Do you believe and trust in his Son Jesus Christ,
 who redeemed mankind?
I believe and trust in him.
Do you believe and trust in his Holy Spirit,
 who gives life to the people of God?
I believe and trust in him.

The symbolism of baptism was very powerful for me: going under the water meant dying to the old, and coming up out of the water meant being raised into new life in Christ. It was a joy to then be welcomed by the whole church family. There was nothing in Buddhism that compared to this. This truly was an answer to the strong desire I'd had in the temple to be baptized, to be in church and to pray. These things were being fulfilled.

Unexpectedly, in the summer of 1992, I received an invitation from Jackie to her wedding in Hong Kong later that year.

She was going to marry John To, who had been a heroin addict for fourteen years and had been greatly helped by God through Jackie's ministry. I couldn't believe I had been invited, and I really wanted to go. After praying, I wrote back to Jackie saying I'd love to come and asking if it would be possible for me to stay an extra three weeks after the wedding so that I could also help in a 'new boy' house (where Chinese men were withdrawing from drugs), as I really wanted to be part of the work first-hand too. She agreed.

It was no small thing to plan a trip to Hong Kong, but it all fell into place very well and before I knew it, I was there being welcomed by one of Jackie's helpers at the airport. I couldn't believe I was in Hong Kong! The heat hit me as I arrived, reminding me of my time in Bangkok. Soon after my arrival I was told that an itinerary had been planned for my month's stay and that I would indeed be helping in a new boy house after the wedding. This was really good news.

For the first week, I stayed in Hang Fook camp. This was a large centre in the middle of a built-up area in Kowloon, made up primarily of single-storey 'huts' that the Hong Kong Housing Department had offered to Jackie to use. All kinds of people lived here, including helpers and those who had withdrawn from drugs. The camp was buzzing with extra people who had come for the wedding, including some from other countries like me. They were all very friendly and glad to be there. There was great excitement in the air and lots of preparations going on.

It was the most amazing wedding I have ever been to in my life! There were so many people there. Jackie had invited her friends, from the street-sleepers and poor of Hong Kong to wealthier people from other countries. For the poor she had provided new clothes, showers and haircuts if they needed them, and she had reserved for them the best seats in the front rows. Those who had travelled from other countries had to find their own seats. The poor, too, were invited to the first and best of the banquet. It was all so biblical!

It was so deeply moving to be there. I could feel God's presence powerfully with us: here were former drug addicts, criminals, street-sleepers, many Chinese and people from all over the world, an incredible assortment of those who had been given new life and hope by Jesus, now as one, worshipping together. Even the most lost and hopeless ones redeemed, including me. God was showing me what is possible for him to do. My heart filled with love for him and for those around me; from time to time it broke me and all I could do was weep.

After the wedding, I was able to go and live in a new boy house for three weeks. This is a first-stage house where male Chinese drug addicts come to live and be prayed off drugs. It was a very beautiful place, a house by the sea on the south of Hong Kong Island that the Chinese government had given permission for Jackie to use. There was a very kind German house leader, about fourteen Chinese brothers and five helpers. The atmosphere in the house was great, with a deep sense of God's love and presence among us. The brothers generally were so sweet and protective, a bunch of really nice lads, so much so that it was hard to remember they had been heroin addicts (some for over fifteen years) and many had been criminals. Most of them had only just withdrawn or were still in the process of withdrawing from drugs.

We lived together like a family, taking care of one another, eating together, cleaning and repairing the house, worshipping twice a day (it was so inspiring to see these men singing their hearts out to God), and going out for recreation times which included playing football, going fishing, swimming or canoeing. The male helpers lived in dormitories with the men coming off drugs, and the women had their own little dormitory with a shower and bathroom. I slept in a bunk bed, as did most of us.

One of our important duties as helpers was to be constantly with a brother (drug addict) when he first arrived at the house. The new arrivals would be dressed in pyjamas for the first few days (so that they could be easily identified if they tried to run away) as they withdrew from drugs. We would take turns of four-hour periods (called 'new boy duty'). We were to pray in tongues or read the Bible and stay close to them, giving no medication or methadone at all, only prayer. Yet over these first few days, all of them miraculously withdrew from the various drugs and/or alcohol to which they had been addicted, through Jesus, and most of them without any pain. If they did start to show signs of pain or discomfort, we would pray for them and they would calm down and the pain would lift. It was extraordinary. I saw these men being changed by God in front of my very eyes.

I loved doing the 'new boy duties'. The brothers were so open to receiving prayer, and I felt totally protected by God's love. One early morning, about 4am, I was praying for a brother who looked very ill. He had been close to death before coming to us. As I prayed for him, he thanked me. It made me feel so humble. What a privilege to be with him at such a vulnerable time in his life and to see God's love for him. Jesus was completely right when he said, 'The thief comes only to steal and kill and destroy; I have come that they may have life, and have it to the full' (John 10:10). Here was this scripture being lived before me.

As my stay progressed, I was aware that it is so easy at times *not* to notice God's miracles, as they are so totally 'natural'. It seemed so natural that these men withdrew painlessly from heroin as we prayed time after time – so much so that I prayed to 'see' the miracles, so that I could thank God for them and not take them for granted.

I was aware, too, that I literally had to 'live' and 'breathe' Jesus to survive here. In my own strength I couldn't offer much. What could I do to help these drug addicts? I'd be terrified! But by praying and calling out to Jesus, he gave us everything we needed, again and again.

Before I left Hong Kong, Jackie prayed for me and thanked God that he had 'bypassed my mind and touched my spirit'. Her words really helped me to understand what had happened to me. Buddhist meditation uses the mind as the main way to try to understand truth and escape suffering. Its strong hold over me had been primarily over my mind and it blinded me to the truth. 'Even if our gospel is veiled, it is veiled to those who are perishing. The god of this age has blinded the minds of unbelievers' (2 Corinthians 4:3–4a). But God had touched my spirit by his Holy Spirit, he had awakened it and his life was born in me. That's what it means to be a Christian; to be alive in our spirits. That's why I could suddenly see that God and his Word, the Bible, are real and I could no longer deny that he exists, having previously regarded it all as a load of nonsense. The Spirit himself testified with my spirit that I was God's child (see Romans 8:16), then wonderfully God started to renew my mind ('the mind controlled by the Spirit is life and peace', Romans 8:6). He now dwelled in me in order to transform me. Buddhists are still dead in their spirits, not having been awakened yet by God's Spirit. Through meditation they try hopelessly to detach from the world of which they are an integral and essential part.

I so enjoyed the trip to Hong Kong. I returned to England really inspired, and continued under the direction and guidance of Will and Rosemary. I felt that I was being prepared for something – but I wasn't sure what.

I kept in touch with Jackie by letter and she gave me much encouragement. Some people commented that one day I would go back to help full time in Hong Kong. Even though I had so enjoyed my time, having lived under spiritual deception for so long, I had no intention of going anywhere unless I was sure it was God's will for my life.

Finally, the three years of waiting were nearly up and I was beginning to feel a change: the Lord was preparing to send me out. I had told him that I would go wherever he sent me, but I didn't yet know where that was.

I wrote to Jackie about this, and she wrote back inviting me to pray and think about joining them in Hong Kong. I was delighted. However, even with the invitation and the thrill of it all, I needed more evidence that this was God's will for me, so I asked some close friends, including Will and Rosemary, to pray in confidence for me about this. God's voice can get cluttered out amid the 'noises' of other people's thoughts and expectations, so it needed to be handled with care.

All of them confirmed that they felt this was God's will for me, and I felt that in my heart too. God's timing had been perfect. I had been in a rush from the beginning, but he knew the best time for me to go. Actually, in the end, it felt as if it was all coming together only within seconds of me being ready! At times, when what was about to happen dawned on me, I felt quite fearful. Would I cope? How would it be living so far from home? Was I ready? I shared my fears with some friends and they prayed for me, which gave me great strength. Someone encouraged me by sharing a scripture: 'Have I not commanded you? Be strong and of good courage; do not be afraid, nor be dismayed, for the LORD your God is with you wherever you go' (Joshua 1:9 NKJV).

I knew in my heart then that he was commanding me to be strong, that there was no place for weakness or excuses. I had to keep my eyes on Jesus, nowhere else, and keep moving forward into his will for me. I was happy to write back to Jackie, saying that I agreed to come and work with St Stephen's Society for a minimum of two years.

Before I left for Hong Kong, I went back to my former temple with two older Christian friends. I met the nun with whom I had ordained, the one who had been so concerned for me. It was good to see her and as soon as she saw me she said, 'Now I know that you made the right decision.' (A few years later she too was to disrobe, not because she had become a Christian, but from disillusionment. Many of the monks and nuns with whom I lived have since disrobed, for various reasons.)

I couldn't believe that I was going to start life as a full-time helper in Jackie's ministry. Finally, after having given my life to Buddha for so long, I was able to go and serve God full time. It felt completely right and the fulfilment of a deep desire, and I can say that from the moment I first disrobed I never regretted it. I never looked back, only forward to more adventures and becoming in him.

13 To Hong Kong

The proclaiming of Jesus will do its own work . . . even if your listeners seem to pay it no attention, they will never be the same again. If I share my own words, they are of no more importance than your words are to me. But if we share the truth of God with one another, we will encounter it again and again. We have to focus on the great point of spiritual power – the Cross. If we stay in contact with that centre of power, its energy is released in our lives. (Oswald Chambers[1])

Just before I left for Hong Kong, I unexpectedly heard from two Buddhist monks from my former temple, one of whom I knew quite well. They happened to be staying nearby and asked if they could visit me. I immediately said 'yes' and invited them for breakfast at my house the next morning. I quickly called my two Christian friends, who looked like innocent older ladies but were powerhouses of intercession, and asked them to join us. Having visited the temple with me, they were excited to come.

The monks arrived in the morning in their saffron robes and we gave them a great breakfast with the best coffee, fruit, cakes and goodies, and I knew how much they appreciated it. As a result, the monks became very relaxed. They were talking a lot about the monastery, and I was beginning to get a bit restless. I was aware that I needed to share Jesus with them, so that they might begin to see their need of him.

Eventually an opening in the conversation came and I managed to tell them about who Jesus was, why he came to earth and died on the cross and rose again, and the promise of spending eternity with him.

After I had finished, one of them (who, incidentally, had been a Jehovah's Witness before ordaining as a Buddhist monk) suddenly became very angry. I quickly changed the subject and talked about something else, and he calmed down again. We could see that he had nasty blisters from walking far. My two friends appeared with a bowl of water and asked if they could wash his feet. They didn't know it was an offence for a monk to be touched by a woman, but they were older and inoffensive, and this was in public, so he agreed. They went ahead and gently washed his feet, putting plasters on his blisters. After they had finished we asked if we could pray for them both. They agreed, so my friends prayed a simple prayer for the monks, and off they went.

Six months later, the monk who had become antagonistic during our conversation phoned me up. He said, 'Esther, I've come to know Jesus. What do I do?' I could barely believe my ears. The Lord had touched him, he'd had a powerful revelation of God and had understood much more than the little we'd shared with him.

At this time I had never met another Buddhist monastic who had come to Christ, and so in a sense I had felt very alone in what had happened to me. Talking to this monk was very reassuring. He too had been extremely confused, at times really not knowing what was happening to him. He was surprised – as I had been – that the Buddha's teaching, which for so long had appeared so real and meaningful to him, like a 'solid mountain', had suddenly collapsed into a pile of rubbish compared to knowing Christ. He asked me where it had gone to. I told him that its illusory and deceptive nature had been exposed and now he could see it as it really is. This great illusion of truth opposes God by having as its goal nothingness and no more becoming, which ultimately is nonsense.

Before long he too disrobed and was baptized, which sadly I couldn't attend as I was in Hong Kong. Finally this searching man had found what he had been looking for so earnestly – the truth – and we all rejoiced with him, with much gratitude to God. This was such a great encouragement and help to me.

Finally, at the end of August 1994, I was off to Hong Kong, sent out as part of the Christ Church Mission Fund team. This was a dream come true for me. Revd Will, Rosemary and some close friends prayed for me during the last Sunday morning service before I left. It was wonderful to go with the blessing of the whole church. I knew it was an enormous step: this time I was going there to live, not just visiting.

Someone shared a scripture with me which was a great encouragement. It was Isaiah 55:12:

For you shall go out with joy,
And be led out with peace;
The mountains and the hills
Shall break forth into singing before you,
And all the trees of the field shall clap their hands.
(NKJV)

On my arrival at the airport in Hong Kong, one of Jackie's helpers came to meet me. It was a comfort having someone there to greet me. She took me to Hang Fook camp, which was somewhere familiar, and I stayed there for the first couple of weeks. There were a few other new helpers arriving at that time, from various parts of the world, so we were to have a short time of training together before going off to various houses. One of them was from England and, being a similar age to me, she soon became a good friend, which was a great support. At the training Jackie came to pray for us and encourage us, and it was great to see her again.

I was really happy when I heard that I would be going back to the same new boy house by the sea that I had been in before. I had many joyful and profound memories of being there. After I moved in, there was a lot of adjusting to do – a new culture (Chinese and St Stephen's), climate, food (many delicious Chinese dishes, but the occasional challenge for me such as chicken's feet!) and language. I couldn't speak Chinese and often didn't really know what was going on. Also at times I felt homesick. Perhaps this is what culture shock means.

I was strongly helped and sustained by the prayers of friends back home, as well as those of the brothers and sisters in the house. At my core, however, I was delighted to be there and expectant for what would happen; seeing the brothers getting free from drugs and growing in daily life made it all worthwhile. At times I thought I should pinch myself to see if it was real. What a lot had changed in the last three years.

As helpers we would regularly attend the drug addicts' meetings held not too far away, in another part of Hong Kong, to meet brothers and pray for the addicts, sometimes bringing one or two back to live with us in the new boy house. These meetings were extraordinary and often the room was absolutely full of people high on heroin or other drugs. Many came along because they had seen their friends changed through Jesus and they too were longing for change. The first time I went, I thought it would be terrifying to be shut in a room full of addicts! There were about thirty of them and the man sitting next to me smelled so strongly of alcohol that I wasn't too sure I'd be able to take it. The room was painted white and all the lights were on. At least, I thought, there was some light in there among all the spiritual darkness! I sat where I could see the door, ready for flight. However, once we started to worship, the atmosphere in the room changed completely. Jesus was here among us and a lightness, a peacefulness and a sense of safety pervaded. I felt slightly embarrassed at myself that I had felt so 'chicken' and had even prepared my escape route.

It was glorious to be here. Jackie was right: his love and grace are special for the very needy ones of the world. He was here, pouring out his love, healing, hope and mercy to these broken people, some of whom were close to death from their long-term addictions. Here he would touch, heal, restore and give life to many. In these meetings, the addicts would say 'yes' to Jesus again and again to receive him into their lives, even in their blurry, drugged state. Spiritual things are spiritually discerned: in their spirits, they knew he was real, even if in their minds they couldn't figure it all out. Here the addicts received the gift of tongues, and they would use it to call out to God for help even when they were still on drugs. They would see Jesus in the eyes of the helpers, receive his touch through the laying on of hands and receive his hope from their prayers and words of encouragement. Their needy souls could finally find rest. What a privilege to sit here and see God descend among us like this and to see lives so deeply changed. I was astounded; I had never experienced anything like it before. I never again felt afraid to go to a drug addicts' meeting and each time I went I would see him come and bless these ones and all of us present.

For years, as a Buddhist, I had believed that Christians were so limited in their outlook, saying that 'Jesus is the only way'. However, once I had come to believe in him myself and 'stepped through the narrow gate', I realized that God had brought me into an incredibly spacious place. The only reason why it was narrow to step through was so that I could leave all my idols and baggage outside. Since disrobing, I have wanted to really embrace and enjoy life to the full, doing the things I enjoy most, such as horse riding, walking in the countryside and along the beach, bird watching, swimming, exercising in the park and having holidays with friends. Now I see life as something to be celebrated, a real adventure.

Buddha was desperately looking for a way out of suffering. He focused all his energies on escaping from old age, sickness and death, which actually ended up in him ultimately wanting to escape from existence itself. By contrast, Christ came to help us to embrace life in its fullness. He embraced his own humanity and never tried to escape it or reject it, and he teaches us to do the same. The things to escape are sin and disobedience to God. Finally, after all those years of antagonism, I could accept and see that Christians are not narrow-minded after all.

Many of the addicts had a Buddhist past, often mixed in with the worship of Chinese idols, ancestor worship and other forms of the occult. They never ceased to be fascinated to hear how God had used them, through a video, to draw me out of Buddhism to himself. The healings and restoration of lives that I witnessed during my time with St Stephen's Society contrasted greatly with my experience in the Buddhist temple. I had never seen the spiritual power in Buddhism to set people free as I was seeing here. The Bible is true when it says that idols – the works of people's hands – are dead and lifeless, but God is alive to heal and restore.

> For the practices of the peoples are worthless;
> they cut a tree out of the forest,
> and a skilled worker shapes it with a chisel.
> They adorn it with silver and gold;
> they fasten it with hammer and nails
> so it will not totter.
> Like a scarecrow in a melon patch,
> their idols cannot speak;
> they must be carried
> because they cannot walk.
> (Jeremiah 10:3–5)

My seventy-eight-year-old father told the family that he would be going out to Hong Kong for my first Christmas in 1994. Mum and my two brothers (one being my stepbrother from Australia) came too and I booked Christmas lunch in a lovely hotel so that we could all celebrate together. During their stay, Mum and Dad had the opportunity to meet Jackie for themselves. They had great respect for her, always feeling that it was because of Jackie that I had left the temple – even though I tried to explain that it was God who got me out by using Jackie. I felt a bit nervous about this meeting, knowing how my parents felt about God. However, Jackie was very welcoming and the three of us went to see her in her office at Hang Fook camp. My mum was able to express from her heart the gratitude she felt towards Jackie for the part she played in my disrobing; it was a very touching and tender moment.

At one point Jackie started to ask Dad about his Christian experience. Dad started off on the same track that he usually did: that he had been forced to go to church on a Sunday as a boy, that it had made him resentful and he never felt he got anything from the church (he didn't tell her about the money he used to steal from the offering bag). Jackie replied with much wisdom, 'It may have put you off the church, but I hope it didn't turn you away from God.' He was silent, he had no reply. After some more chatting, we left Jackie's office. We were all very quiet, each one of us deep in our own thoughts, having been blessed and challenged in different ways. After meeting Jackie, my parents continued to speak with very high regard for her and for St Stephen's Society.

I didn't know it at the time, of course, but Dad's visit to Hong Kong was the last time I would ever see him. Six months later, quite unexpectedly, he passed away peacefully from a stroke.

As time passed, I started to feel that there might be something new on the horizon. As much as I was greatly blessed by being part of St Stephen's Society, I sensed deep down that it was not a long-term calling. Many of the foreign helpers had done very well in learning Chinese, but I felt lazy and not that concerned to do it, which I thought was telling me something. I prayed a prayer that Jackie encouraged us to pray if we felt ready for it. (Please beware that if you pray this prayer, you will need to be ready for change, as it may well open up new doors in your life.) The prayer went something like this: 'Father, please touch my heart with something of your heart for the people you are calling me to.' I prayed, not really knowing who those people were, but before long that prayer was to be answered.

14 The call to Thailand

For every civilization, for every period of history, it is true to say: 'show me what kind of gods you have, and I will tell you what kind of humanity you possess.'
(Emil Brunner[1])

Not long after praying that prayer, I started thinking a lot about Thailand, a place I had barely thought about during the last few years. At one point, nearly every time I began to worship, I saw pictures in my mind of miracles of healing among the Thai people, with many thousands of them coming to Christ, throwing away their idols and Buddha images into big piles. Eventually I spoke to Jackie about this and she said, 'I think the Lord is preparing you for Thailand.'

With this in mind, not long afterwards, in December 1995, Jackie sent me and a friend, an English helper from Hong Kong, on a short-term mission trip to Thailand. This was the first of several short trips over the next few years. I was keen to get to know the situation of the Thai church better, and was greatly helped by being able to meet some Thai church leaders and missionaries. I hadn't been back to Thailand since deciding to become a Buddhist nun up in the north-east, some ten years before.

I remember one day standing on a street corner in Bangkok. I was aware that people in countries like England often find it difficult to relate to my testimony of coming out of Buddhist monasticism: to them it is just an interesting but strange story. In Thailand, however, where 93% of the population are Theravada Buddhists (it is the national religion) and only 1% are Christian, it is really relevant. Suddenly it all made sense. This was what God had been preparing me for, and for the first time I could see why God had allowed me to go so deeply into Buddhism: he was using my life's experiences to lay a foundation for the call he was giving me to Thailand and to Buddhists. My past had been and was being redeemed by God for his purposes. I felt like a secret agent with a deep understanding of Buddhism that the average Thai in the street had no idea I possessed! God was beginning to equip and authorize me to minister to those stuck in the same bondages that had ensnared me.

A deep desire arose in me to learn to speak, read and write Thai. I started to be fascinated by the language. As a nun I had never been interested to learn it, even though I had often been surrounded by Thai monks and nuns. Now I really wanted to and immediately bought some children's writing books and a Thai alphabet, and started practising my letters.

Around that time too, Thai people started to stand out as 'special' for me, in that God gave me a deep love for the people which has lasted for many years now. It's not that I don't care for people from other nations, as I do, but the Thais definitely stand out for me. I have a greater urgency and desire to see Thai Christians mature, grow and be strengthened in their faith, and I long to see the lives of Thai Buddhists transformed by coming to know Christ. Perhaps this was an answer to the prayer that I prayed in Hong Kong that God would touch my heart with something of his heart for the people he was calling me to.

Coming back to Thailand as a Christian was now so interesting for me, and it was as if I was seeing the Thais with fresh eyes. Often I felt I could see that the radiance of many people's faces was dulled – dulled by the bondage of idolatry. I hadn't noticed this before. It was literally like a 'veil' over some of their faces. Scripture tells us that we become like the thing we worship, and that idols are by nature dead and lifeless. I was now seeing this truth for myself.

> Their idols are silver and gold,
> made by human hands.
> They have mouths, but cannot speak,
> eyes, but cannot see.
> They have ears, but cannot hear,
> noses, but cannot smell.
> They have hands, but cannot feel,
> feet, but cannot walk,
> nor can they utter a sound with their throats.
> Those who make them will be like them,
> and so will all who trust in them.
> (Psalm 115:4–8)

I was still living in Hong Kong when I was invited to spend a month in Mongolia during August 1996. I went with a small team from Hong Kong, to help members of a German church which was doing long-term outreach there. After praying, I felt I should go, but really wasn't sure why. We were based in a small town, Hinti, twelve hours by van east of the capital Ulan Bator, and were living in Mongolian tents. It was quite an adventure!

We were sent out most days in five or six teams of three or four people, including a Mongolian translator. We took food and clothes to the poor as well as sharing about Jesus. I was interested to discover that some Mongolian people believed in Tibetan Buddhism. I trained myself not to look at the idols and shrines as I entered their tents or houses, but to keep my 'spiritual eyes' on Jesus. What we witnessed in our various teams was astounding. Many whole families of Mongolian people whom we told about Jesus came to believe in him, day after day, often with miracles of healing and the baptism of the Holy Spirit occurring too. This didn't happen just to the team of a particularly gifted evangelist, but to nearly every team sent out. I saw for myself, for the first time, a whole family of Buddhists come to Christ; they were so hungry to know him. Some of these new believers decided immediately to get rid of their idols and Buddhist amulets. This is a sure sign of clear conversion to Christ. (Some people continue to keep hold of them for a while, just in case their new God doesn't work – a bit like an insurance policy!)

One Mongolian man who came to Christ when we visited his family immediately received this powerful insight: 'Buddhism is only an idea in the mind, there is no truth in it.' He was absolutely right. He had been a Tibetan Buddhist, but the minute he believed in Jesus, the deception, blindness and bondage were broken off from his mind.

This short-term mission trip turned out to be such a powerful encouragement. To see Buddhists coming to Christ like this really revealed to me his hope for what was possible in Thailand. I had seen it with my own eyes. Flying home to Hong Kong, I now understood why God had wanted me to go to Mongolia!

My heart and thoughts continued to be with Thailand, even though I wasn't living there yet, so I was glad when I could go for another short visit in March 1998. By this time I was sure God was calling me to go and live there and it was just a matter of time. On this trip, we went into a slum with a lovely Thai Christian friend, Noi, who worked with the many poor living in Bangkok slums. We went to visit a friend of Noi's who lived in a shoddily made shelter on top of a rubbish dump.

As we were sitting chatting, with a couple of small children crawling around by our feet, we noticed the presence of a very withdrawn lady, maybe about thirty years old. She was so withdrawn that she was almost like a 'non-presence' – where it felt as if she was almost not there at all. She was a drug addict and very ill with AIDS. Her skin was badly marked with pus-filled, runny sores, which made it evident that she was in the late stages of the disease.

Noi and I knew that we really needed to share about Jesus with her. We asked her if she knew who Jesus was, and she didn't. We started to tell her and made sure she understood. Then Noi asked her if she would like to know him. She said, 'Yes.' She prayed in Thai to receive Jesus into her life. Her body was very dry, very desiccated, but these two little tears welled up in her eyes and the presence of the Lord was such that it was as if he was standing there with us. A Bible verse came to my mind, that 'neither height nor depth, nor anything else in all creation, will be able to separate us from the love of God' (Romans 8:39).

Here was this terribly fearful woman, suffering from AIDS, ravaged by drug addiction, dying, and not knowing God. But Jesus came to meet her, and after she received him into her life her countenance changed, she really came alive. We really do come alive when we know that we're going to spend eternity with God and that he has forgiven us for all our sins. We were so blessed by it all that we seemed to 'fly' out of that slum when we left! I wouldn't have known what hope to give her if it wasn't for Christ. It's such a tremendous privilege to know him and to be able to take him to others.

I shared this story with a Thai Christian friend called Malee, and she had some interesting comments. 'This drug addict lady's state of non-presence and withdrawal represents the state of most Thai Buddhists who believe they don't have a self. That's why so many people feel worthless and bound; no freedom to express themselves properly. It's almost like their spirits are crushed. So people like Noi's friend who was on the fringe of society felt even more worthless, like she didn't even have a right to exist. Such beliefs go against their true nature as God made them to be. Buddhism denies the very God-given nature that we have and it takes so much effort to suppress what God has created, to live as if they don't have a self. So when people get free through Jesus, we often see such joy and their true identities and personalities emerge. It's as if they have escaped from a prison.'

After three years in Hong Kong, I left St Stephen's Society and returned to the UK. I was extremely grateful for my time and experiences there. I have been back to visit a few times since then, sometimes popping in to see the brothers and sisters there. When I was there recently, I saw one of the former drug addicts I had met in the new boy house during my first year. He looked so well and so clear in his faith. He was surprised and happy to see me, and said, 'Esther, the last ten years have been the best ten years of my life!'

He is one of literally thousands of lives that God has touched and changed through St Stephen's Society – including mine. Overall it was a period of tremendous growth for me, with much of Jackie's teaching laying an important foundation in my Christian life. However, I realized that it had been a training ground and that Thailand was now 'home'. I needed to move on.

15 Life as a missionary in Thailand

Christ loved the church and gave himself for her, that he might
sanctify and cleanse her with the washing of water by the word,
that he might present her to himself a glorious church, not
having spot or wrinkle or any such thing, but that she should
be holy and without blemish.
(Ephesians 5: 25b–27 NKJV)

I finally arrived to live in Thailand full time as a missionary
late in 1999. The time from leaving Hong Kong to going to
Thailand seemed to pass by very quickly. Wonderfully, I
continued to be sent out and supported by Christ Church
(which was now led by a new vicar and his wife, Revd Dave
and Lois). Their prayers, love and support had helped to
sustain me in Hong Kong and I knew I looked to them and
other praying friends for continued support in what lay ahead.

I felt that being in Thailand could hold a greater challenge,
as I was going right back into a country where the national
religion was exactly the one from which the Lord had freed
me. The effects of centuries of Buddhism go very deep in
Thai culture and society, often permeating the language,
thinking and behaviour. I had seen the effects of Theravada

Buddhism on me as an individual, and now I was about to see its effects on a nation. My past personal involvement with it was to become a great help in beginning to understand those effects. I held a great confidence in my heart too: if God could free me from Buddhism, he could definitely help people in Thailand.

I wasn't sure how long I would be there, but I was willing to go for as long as God wanted me there. I had settled that with him before leaving.

Once in Thailand, I felt that I had finally *arrived*, after years of being in situations where I was just passing through to get to somewhere else (wherever that was). I suddenly felt that I was home. For the first time in my life I bought things for my apartment, such as furniture, a washing machine, a fridge and other things that showed I was settling down. It was quite a challenge, as I realized this was a serious and long-term commitment. For once I wasn't, in the back of my mind, preparing to move on.

The feeling of familiarity was helped by having spent some time in the country before, prior to ordaining as a nun, and having lived 'Thai style' in the Buddhist temple in England. I started to wonder also if a strong bond with Asia had actually developed for me during my childhood years in Singapore.

My first year in Bangkok was spent at language school, learning Thai. Assisted by much prayer, slowly my ability to read, write and speak Thai started to develop. This was truly amazing as I am not a linguist and I knew God was helping me in an extraordinary way. It was like having a second 'Thai' childhood as I learned to copy the strange and wonderful shapes that make up the Thai alphabet. The various squiggles fascinated me, and still do. Our Thai language teachers became like surrogate mothers, teaching us patiently how to say these strange sounds, smiling and encouraging us when we got them right. Learning a second language when you are older can be a humbling process!

It wasn't all easy, though – it was and still is sometimes hard to come to terms with living in such a different culture. The Thais were not like the Chinese people I had become more used to. Chinese people in Hong Kong tend to be very expressive and really speak out what they think. Thais are gentle, polite people who don't want to hurt other people's feelings, so they are very cautious in how they express themselves so as not to offend. This sometimes makes it really hard to know how they actually feel or what they are trying to say. Sometimes they say what they think the other person wants to hear. In the early days I often felt confused in relating to them, realizing that I had a lot to learn about this very different culture and complex social system.

I had been in Thailand for about two years when I met up with Hope Taylor again. Hope had kindly come to visit me when I was preparing to become a Buddhist nun in the temple in the north-east of Thailand in 1983. She was over the moon that I had become a Christian, and was fascinated to hear my story. I had a deep sense of gratitude and respect towards her. Amazingly, now we had similar interests regarding the Thai church we became good friends – such a contrast to our previous meeting!

Since arriving in Thailand, I have been based in a Thai church in the central part of the country and have been involved in a Christian ministry that has discipleship as its core theme. The work ranges from helping Thai church leaders to mature and grow in Christ to helping the newest Christians develop in their faith. We work interdenominationally with the Thai churches, usually in teams. Many of the team members are Thais, but some foreign missionaries come along to help too. I really enjoy our travels to the provinces, when we visit and encourage believers. Thailand is such a beautiful country and the people are very welcoming and hospitable. My world is very 'Thai'. I eat Thai food most days, which is great. Many of my close friends are Thai, and

I worship in a Thai church. I enjoy standing alongside my Thai brothers and sisters in church on a Sunday morning. Sometimes I stop singing just to listen, and I think, 'If that sound is sweet to me, how much sweeter must it be to the Lord?'

We live by faith, which Jackie taught me to do, so we pray for finances, both for the ministry and for personal needs. I have seen God's faithfulness and provision over many years now, for which I am truly grateful. Recently we needed a car, so we prayed along with several friends – and wonderfully were given a large sum of money so that we could buy one. We never seem to lack the things that we need!

Of all the things that I've done in my life, the one thing about which I could have felt a sense of regret is having wasted so many years as a Buddhist nun. Yet coming back to Thailand and serving God among Buddhists has redeemed that sense of loss. In God's economy, it seems, nothing is wasted. He can use it all.

Although Thailand is richer than some of its neighbouring countries, we face many challenges. We have widespread problems with drug and alcohol addiction, poverty, corruption, injustice and prostitution (of men, women and children). People often ask me why I think there is so much prostitution in Thailand. Do I think the reason is poverty? I would say that is the polite answer. However, I believe the real root cause is idolatry. Idolatry and sexual immorality seem to be virtually inseparable; where you find one, you will nearly always find the other. This connection is spoken of in the Bible:

[They] exchanged the glory of the immortal God for images made to look like mortal human beings and birds and animals and reptiles. Therefore God gave them over in the sinful desires of their hearts to sexual impurity . . . They exchanged the truth about God for a lie, and worshipped

and served created things rather than the Creator . . . God
gave them over to a depraved mind, so that they do what
ought not to be done.
(Romans 1:22–28)

I have seen this happen. As a person's gaze comes off God
and fixes on an idol – any created thing – and as they begin
to worship there, it's as if God steps back and gives their mind
over to perverse, unclean thinking. Possibilities that someone
would never even have considered, had they not strayed from
worshipping God, now become a reality and, even worse,
desirable. It's as if God's hand of protection lifts from them
to let sin run its course. Finally, the person is enslaved by
those perverse desires, bound like a fly in a spider's web,
which was never God's intention had they kept their eyes
on him.

Very sadly, some Thai families sell their children into
prostitution. In some of the poorer villages in the provinces
theirs may be among the nicest houses in the village, bought
with the earnings from their child's prostitution. For most
people, this would be absolutely unthinkable. I don't say
this to condemn, but to try to understand what's happening.
Even to be able to contemplate doing such a thing has, I
believe, spiritual roots.

Paradoxically, many Thai prostitutes are actually very
'religious'. Often they are Buddhist, but they may worship
other gods and spirits too. I was interested to read Alex
Smith who said, 'wherever Buddhism spread, it had a vacuum
cleaner effect, sucking up indigenous religions under its
broad umbrella.'[1] Some of the large and well-used shrines to
idols have been built where the prostitutes work, emphasiz-
ing the point that idolatry and immorality are often closely
linked. As individuals or nations fall into idolatry, morality
can decline to the point where some won't even know what
it is any more.

I have found it fascinating to see how people's beliefs affect their behaviour as individuals and even as a nation. For instance, the Buddhist belief in karma has a strong impact on many Thai people's treatment of living things. Strictly speaking, it is considered a sin to kill any kind of sentient being, so some Buddhists will try never even to kill vermin, such as cockroaches, rats and rabid dogs. Some go to the point of not putting bleach down the drains in case something perishes. Thailand is a hot, tropical country and has lots of vermin. This is really dangerous for spreading diseases, but the ideal of not killing is often held more highly than the safety aspect because of the fear of acquiring bad karma. In contrast, God told us to 'have dominion . . . over every living thing that moves on the earth' (Genesis 1:28 NKJV), which in my thinking means that we need to be good and responsible stewards, but frees us from the idea that we need to be friends with vermin!

Recently I had a very close encounter with this fear of acquiring bad karma. We have numerous wild dogs in Thailand, which have been abandoned, living and breeding in the streets, sometimes in packs. There was a large, aggressive dog that lived outside in my street. It was being fed by the local restaurant owner. One day, when I was walking outside near my house, it quietly came up to me, as if it wanted to greet me, and then, completely unprovoked, bit me on the ankle. I rushed to the local hospital and promptly started a course of ten rabies injections. These were costly and painful. I asked the head of my village to deal with the dog, and she told me that the person feeding it wouldn't agree to have it put down. Even though I asked the government dog catchers to come several times and take the dog away, they never came. I said to the head of my village that they had more respect for dogs than for humans, and she didn't disagree. I felt helpless.

A few weeks later I was out in my street again, talking to my neighbour, and the same dog, having heard and recognized my voice, silently crept up behind me. I didn't even see it this time. It bit my other ankle, this time more aggressively. I was shocked and called Christ Church for prayer from the hospital. This time the wounds were more severe and had to be washed and dressed by a nurse every day for several days as there was a serious risk of infection. They took several weeks to heal. I felt desperate, but fortunately I was about to move house and so I left as quickly as I could! I knew nothing would be done about the dog, and I had failed in my own meagre attempts to kill it.

Belief in the theory of karma can create quite a casual approach to life, which is often treated as cheap. If people believe that their circumstances in life are only the result of past karma and that they have many lives to come, then why not hold it lightly. It can make this life seem less relevant and important. A Thai Christian friend noted recently that she feels such belief also leads easily to people having a lack of responsibility for themselves and for others, such as parents giving their children away for others to raise when they could raise them themselves.

This belief in karma also creates a society that is very respectful towards hierarchy (in society and in Buddhism), due to the belief that some people have earned 'good karma' and some 'bad karma' in a past life. For instance, if you are born poor you must have done something bad in a former life. Such a view results in the feeling that some people deserve more respect and honour than others. This contrasts with the Christian understanding that everyone is equal in God's sight. We are all sinners saved by grace and no-one is higher than another. Even Jesus himself took the lowliest of births. Jesus never spoke of or recognized karma in any way.

I could begin to see the dramatic effect that Buddhism had on the people of Thailand. The result of believing that all things are impermanent, unsatisfactory and 'not belonging to a self' can really affect the way people live and understand their lives. There can often be a lack of ambition in Thai people, as this is seen as a negative thing. Some find it hard to get motivated, or to see things through, sometimes not even bothering to get things done or started at all. 'No need to paint the house, it doesn't matter.' 'Don't bother to fix the flooding of the house, as it only happens once a year.' These are things I have heard people say – as if in the end why bother, if it's all empty and not mine?

It even reaches the point where people are encouraged not to express feelings and emotions very much, as it is considered better not to exhibit such things outwardly. Hence some people show very few facial expressions. This seems to me like a real denial of our humanity. This is in such contrast to the Christian perspective: the 'heart' – referring to both the soul and the spirit in a person – undoubtedly exists and is the centre of our being, the wellspring of life, from which come emotions, thoughts, motivations, courage and action. Proverbs 4:23 says, 'Guard your heart, for it is the wellspring of life.'

The effect of these teachings on people's lives can be quite devastating and debilitating, a bit like taking the backbone out of an individual or society. It can lead to crippling sloth and complacency, dreadful barrenness of heart and spirit, and an erosion of the power of the will, all of which God never intended for us.

This deep inner barrenness is a perfect foundation for addictive behaviour, of which we see much. For example, it is true that Buddha taught that people should not drink alcohol to excess, but sadly he didn't give people an effective way that would enable or empower them to do that, so alcoholism is a big problem in Thailand. Even in most Thai churches there has to be a ban on members drinking alcohol as, even for a believer, to drink in moderation could be hard, such is the vulnerability to addictive behaviour. From what

I have observed, Buddhism doesn't offer a way to help people restrain their sinful desires: rules, human effort and ideals alone are not enough.

In our work, we come across Christian and non-Christian people trapped in various addictions, all of which are a sign of the unacknowledged needy, empty, hurting hearts that long to be recognized, loved and nurtured. Often people struggling with addictions are looking for a way of relief and escape from pain, but in the end addictions provide no true answers and often lead to destruction. We teach about Jesus, who blesses our humanity, affirms us in our being, shares our weaknesses, heals our souls and forgives our sins – the God who is the answer to every problem and longing. I have learned that my role is only to lead each person to Jesus, so that he can help them; I am to keep my eyes on him and let him do it. Wonderfully, we see many Thais and others blessed, healed and freed through God's love and presence, as well as those who turn away from emptiness as their goal and receive life, being and meaning in him.

Another Thai Christian friend said one day that she thought the work we do is a bit like that of a beautician, helping to make the bride of Christ more beautiful and more ready for him, and it seems to be true (see Ephesians 5:25b–27). As Jesus ministers his love, forgiveness and truth to people, they really do become more beautiful. The healing of their souls reflects and shines effortlessly outwards in every aspect of their life, as they are restored by Jesus. Then we see the real beauty and meaning of a human life, as God always intended it to be. Personally, I think the Thai face of the bride of Christ is extremely beautiful. She is small and in the minority, and she is often weak and in need of help, but I see that Christ is totally committed to her, and I'm so grateful for the sense of fulfilment, despite various challenges, that I have felt over the last years serving God here. Church growth was very slow for many years, but now there are many more

Thais coming to know God. It is my great joy to watch God do it. Being here has made sense of my past, all the searching and far wandering, after being redeemed by him, have even become a useful tool in his hands.

Conclusion

'I am the way and the truth and the life.'
(John 14:6)

This is the ultimate reality. When we come to Jesus, the Truth, then the meaning of all things begins to be restored. Truth (*Veritas*) is so beautiful. Apart from it, all meaning, even being itself, is lost. To be unable to glimpse truth, to verbalize it, to see its fullness in all creation, to hope for its fullness in our eternal life, is to know emptiness.
(Leanne Payne[1])

I thank God for the opportunity to write this book, which has been brewing away for several years now. I wanted to write of my Lord who sought me out of the deadening lifestyle of a Buddhist nun and called me into life in him. Every day his presence is with me, and my life now is so different from those many days spent in the Buddhist temple. I hope my story might help and encourage you to realize afresh just how wonderful, powerful and loving God truly is.

I'm so grateful for God's love and persistence with me. Even after he had touched me as a Buddhist nun, and I *still* decided not to follow him, he didn't abandon me, but persisted, until finally from my heart I submitted willingly to him. The fact that he pursued me despite my rebellion and idolatry moves me very deeply and surely reveals something profound to us about his character and nature. He then rescued me from Buddhism and brought me to safety, real purpose and meaning in him. Once I had really come to know God, the Creator, it was simply impossible to follow the philosophy of a created human being, however refined, idealistic and high minded it was. By comparison it became insignificant and redundant.

In all, I was a Buddhist for over thirteen years, and have now been a Christian for more than seventeen years. I thank God that he has given me a deep love for Buddhists. I love the people, but I long to see them set free from Buddhism, to discover the true living God.

It is my firm belief that he is not the one true God for one person only and untrue for another. He is the *only* true God. Jesus died for all. He loves all those who he created, including those who are trapped in Buddhism, and seeks to free them to be able to walk in his ways. The gospel of Christ is the key that will raise us and our nations up out of idolatry, confusion, addiction, corruption, injustice and other forms of suffering. It provides an answer, too, for those nations which are increasingly secular and materialistic, outlooks which ultimately lead to meaninglessness and despair.

Since I was a young woman, I sought truth. Through all the hills, valleys and far landscapes that I've travelled, I have found it wonderfully in him. As the Christian writer Leanne Payne succinctly says, 'All that is good, beautiful, and true comes to us from out of the holiness of God.'[2] A world without him doesn't bear contemplation – a world without truth, beauty, justice, righteousness and all the wonderful things that he is and that he brings to us. To be separate from Jesus is, in the end, to be separate from all that is real and true.

'Blessed are those who are called to the marriage supper of the Lamb!'
(Revelation 19:9 NKJV)

Prayers and pointers for taking things further

Prayer of commitment to Christ
A life of commitment to Jesus Christ means that you:

1. **Acknowledge that you are a sinner and repent of your sin.**
   Romans 3:23: 'For all have sinned and fall short of the glory of God.'
2. **Believe that Christ died on the cross and rose again to save you from your sin and to give you eternal life.**
   John 3:16: 'For God so loved the world that he gave his one and only Son, that whoever believes in him shall not perish but have eternal life.'
3. **Receive Christ by faith and accept the gift God has provided in his Son.**
   John 14:6: 'Jesus answered, "I am the way and the truth and the life. No-one comes to the Father except through me."'
4. **Commit your life to the Lord Jesus Christ and follow him and serve him without reserve.**
   Matthew 16:24: 'Whoever wants to be my disciple must deny themselves and take up their cross and follow me.'

5. **Acknowledge that Jesus now lives in you and through you by his Spirit.**
   Colossians 1:27: 'Christ in you, the hope of glory.'
6. **Are prepared to tell others about Jesus and that you belong to him.**
   Romans 10:9–10: 'If you declare with your mouth, "Jesus is Lord," and believe in your heart that God raised him from the dead, you will be saved. For it is with your heart that you believe and are justified, and it is with your mouth that you profess your faith and are saved.'

If you don't know Jesus yet, but would like to invite him into your life, you can do so now by praying the prayer below. I encourage you after that to get in touch with a local Bible-believing Christian church that can help you continue in your walk with God.

Lord Jesus,
I know that I am a sinner. I turn away from my sin, in repentance, and ask you to forgive me. I believe you died on the cross for my sin and I thank you with all my heart. I now invite you to come into my heart and life. By faith, I receive you as my Saviour, and make you my Lord and Master. I place my whole life in your hands. Thank you that you not only died to give me the gift of eternal life, but you rose again to live your life in me and through me, by your Spirit. I am prepared to acknowledge you as my Lord before others and, in dependence on the Holy Spirit, to live for you in obedience to your promptings. Thank you that according to your Word you have come in and made me your child. Thank you that you have cleansed and forgiven my sin, and given me eternal life. Amen.

Prayer for God's affirmation in your identity and inner being
God created you for himself, for communion with him. If, however, during your life you have felt dreadful feelings of

anxiety, abandonment, emptiness and loneliness, then you can pray or receive prayer for God's affirmation in your identity and inner being. Praying a prayer such as this may help to bring you out of the feeling that you don't exist, into life and life in abundance, which is only from God.

Nobody truly knows who they are until they come into relationship with God. In his presence he names you 'my son' or 'my daughter'. God delights in restoring his children and giving to them the things that they lack. You need his healing presence for this. He will restore to you that true centre in which you can receive love and a sense of being. Finally you can rest, truly knowing who you are and why you were born. Nothing else or nobody else can truly tell you that.

It is good to have a mature, trustworthy Christian pray this through with you.

Heavenly Father,
Like David, who likened his soul to a 'weaned child with his mother'
(Psalm 131:2), I enter into your presence. I acknowledge you,
Father, to be the steadfast and tender One. I come to you seeking
the depth of your affirmation and confirmation at the level for
which you intend it. With the help of the Holy Spirit,
I avail to you the deep-seated dread, fear and anxiety that has
pervaded my life. Envelop me with your loving, steadfast presence.
By your grace, secure in me the very ground of my being that
mother and/or those who nurtured me were somehow unable to
confirm in me. Free me to receive your love, as the Creator and
Redeemer of my life. Become the ground of my security as a person.
Free me to live out of your loving initiative toward me. Amen.[1]

Prayer for renouncing idolatry

The prayer below (or something like it) can be used when renouncing Buddhism or idolatry of various kinds. Ideally it should be prayed under the leadership of a mature Christian, who can also offer a prayer of blessing and cleansing afterwards.

Additionally, any books, Buddha images, statues, amulets, charms, etc. need to be destroyed, ideally before the prayer is said. God needs to see commitment in action as well as words, which is the meaning of true repentance. Each idol should be named before God, renounced and repented of in Jesus' name.

Dear Jesus,
I come to you now and enter into your presence. Before you, I repent of the sin of having been involved in Buddhism. I now renounce it and turn away from it. I choose to worship and give myself to you only, Jesus, and to have no other gods before you. Forgive me for my idolatry, Lord. Now, dear Jesus, wash me clean from the effects of it, and cut and destroy the relationship that I have had with Buddhism so that it no longer has any power or influence over my life. Please wash and renew my mind, help me to see idolatry and detest it as you do, Lord. Help me to keep my mind solely on you. Thank you, Lord Jesus. In your name I pray. Amen.

The person praying with the one renouncing Buddhism/ idolatry might use these words:

Thank You, Lord Jesus, for [name]'s prayer, and that you now stand between [name] and Buddhism. Dear Lord Jesus, please take the sword of the Spirit which is the Word of God and break any relationship and connection that [name] has had with Buddhism so that [he/she] is totally free from it. Wash and cleanse [name] from the effects of Buddhism in [his/her] mind, body, soul and spirit, even in [his/her] subconscious mind. Thank you that you died to set [name] free and that [he/she] is free now. Please fill [name] with your Holy Spirit. Help [him/her] to guard [his/her] mind, renew [his/her] mind and give [him/her] the mind of Christ. Bless your [son/daughter], dear Lord, in [his/her] true self as you have made [him/her] to be. Thank you for the new freedom that [name] has in you now. In Jesus' name. Amen.

Important differences between Christianity and Buddhism

JESUS	BUDDHA
1. Jesus is the Son of **God** (Matthew 3:17).	1. Buddha was a **man**; he never claimed to be a god or God.
2. Jesus is **eternal**. He was with Father God in heaven since the beginning of time and will reign for ever (John 1:1–2).	2. Buddha **lived the lifespan of a man** only, eighty years.
3. Jesus was and is **active in creating the universe**, and is **active in sustaining it** (John 1:3; Colossians 1:16–17).	3. Buddha is **not involved in creating or sustaining the universe**. As a man, he did not have those creative abilities.
4. Jesus **takes us to Father God**, and is the only way to the Father (John 14:6).	4. Buddha **points to emptiness**, and in effect teaches that there is no God.
5. Jesus rose from the dead, **he is alive** (1 Corinthians 15:4) and overcame the power of sin, death and hell.	5. Buddha did not rise from the dead. **He died**.
6. Jesus is the perfect sacrifice for all of humanity's sins as we believe in him. He took on our sins at the cross (Isaiah 53:4–6; 2 Corinthians 5:21; Colossians 2:13–14). Our sins are **atoned** for, we are cleansed and forgiven by the power of the blood of Christ.	6. Buddha, as a man, is **not able to atone**, cleanse or forgive us of our sins.

7. Our wounds and brokenness have a place to go into the wounds of the resurrected Jesus. (Isaiah 53:5; 1 Peter 2:24).

7. Buddha **did not die for our wounds and brokenness**.

8. Jesus is our **Saviour – he brings us to salvation** through his death and resurrection (John 4:42).

8. Buddha is **not a saviour**. Buddha taught that you need to save yourself.

9. Jesus only did the **will of Father God**, and teaches what the Father shows him (John 5:30; 6:38).

9. Buddha taught that which he discovered: it is the **philosophy of man**.

10. Jesus came that we might have **life to the full**, and he taught us how to do that (John 10:10).

10. Buddha taught that **all things are impermanent, unsatisfactory and not self**, and that we need to get out of and escape suffering.

11. Jesus **embraced his life and humanity** (John 10:10).

11. Buddha's goal is **to escape from suffering and ultimately any form of existence**.

12. In Jesus there is always more **becoming** (2 Corinthians 3:18).

12. Buddha taught that the goal is **extinction, non-being**.

13. Jesus became for us our **salvation, redemption, wisdom, righteousness and sanctification** (1 Corinthians 1:30).

13. Buddha did not become for us our salvation, redemption, wisdom, righteousness and sanctification. He told us to **find all these things ourselves**.

CHRISTIANS

1. Christians have a real, vital, living relationship with God. We know God and he knows us. **Christianity is relational** (John 14:20).

2. Christians have **Christ living in them** by the Holy Spirit. 'Christ in you, the hope of glory' (Colossians 1:27).

3. Christians are **alive in their spirits** (Romans 8:11).

4. Christians conceive **truth in their spirits** (John 4:24).

5. Christians find their **'true self'** through Jesus, who gives life meaning and purpose (Romans 8:28).

6. Christians **enjoy** life, 'ever more becoming' as they remain in Jesus (John 10:10).

7. Christians **pray** to God (Matthew 6:9).

BUDDHISTS

1. Buddhists **do not have a personal relationship with Buddha**. You are not knowing someone or being known by them.

2. Buddhists **do not have Buddha living in them**.

3. Buddhists are **not alive in their spirits**.

4. Buddhists essentially **try to find truth through their minds**.

5. Buddhism uses self-effort to try and realize that **there is no self**.

6. Buddhists have as their goal **an end of any becoming at all**.

7. Buddhists **don't pray** to God. Meditation is not the same as prayer. (You can't pray to 'nothingness' or a philosophy, and even though some Asian Buddhists have deified Buddha, he never taught his followers to do that.)

CHRISTIANITY TEACHES	BUDDHISM TEACHES
1. **God created the world**, so it is good to embrace it (Genesis 1:1).	1. **Ignorance created the world**, so it is better to escape it.
2. **Do not worship idols** or make an image of God (Exodus 20:1–6).	2. The original teaching of Buddha teaches not to worship idols, but over time **many idols of Buddha have been made and worshipped**.
3. The **Trinity** of Father God, Jesus the Son and the Holy Spirit (John 3:34; Matthew 28:19).	3. There is **no God**, only the philosophy of man.
4. **The love of beauty** as God created it (Genesis 1:31).	4. **All things are impermanent and unsatisfactory**, including beauty.
5. **Live life** to the full (in a godly way) (John 10:10).	5. **Detach from the world**, don't attach to it.
6. What **justice, righteousness, obedience and sin** truly are (Psalm 89:14).	6. **Does not truly define justice, righteousness and sin**, as a man is not fully capable of doing this, but only the Creator.
7. Suffering came into the world through the fall. **Jesus can meet us in our suffering** and use it for his glory (Isaiah 61:1–3).	7. **The need to find the way out of suffering**.

8. Empowerment by Jesus to live in righteousness and obedience, through his **Holy Spirit** (Matthew 28:19).

8. Trying to live well by **self-effort**.

9. How to **embrace our humanity** (John 10:10).

9. See our **humanity as something not to attach to**.

10. **Eternal life** for all those who confess Jesus as their Lord and Saviour and live in righteousness, and **hell** for those who don't (John 3:16–18; Luke 12:5).

10. **'Karma'**, or a cycle of rebirth, i.e. into the human, animal or hungry ghost realm, and the goal of non-being.

11. Salvation is a **free gift** from God. We just have to accept his invitation; there is nothing we can do to earn it (Ephesians 2:4–5).

11. Rules and regulations need to be kept as a vehicle to the goal and merit has to be **earned** by self-effort.

Further reading

G. K. Beale, *We Become What we Worship: A Biblical Theology of Idolatry*, IVP Academic, 2008.

Oswald Chambers, *My Utmost for His Highest*, Classic Edition, Barbour Publishing Inc., 1963.

Leanne Payne, *Restoring the Christian Soul*, Baker Books, 1997.

Leanne Payne, *The Healing Presence*, Baker Books, 1997.

Rebecca Manley Pippert, *Out of the Saltshaker*, IVP, 1999.

Jackie Pullinger, *Crack in the Wall*, Hodder and Stoughton, London, 1989.

Jackie Pullinger, *Chasing the Dragon*, Hodder and Stoughton, 1980.

Alex G. Smith, *Buddhism through Christian Eyes*, OMF International, 2001.

Websites

www.uk.alphacourse.org   For those interested to find out more about Jesus.

www.oswaldchambers.co.uk   Thoughtful books for daily devotion and general Christian life.

www.leannepayne.org   For books and courses in developing our relationship with Christ.

www.estherbaker.com   For further information and to contact the author.

Notes

Epigraph

1. Leanne Payne, referring to Charles Williams, *Descent into Hell*, Wm. B. Eerdmans Publishing Co., 1949, in *Real Presence*, Hamewith Books, 1997, p. 154.

Chapter 3

1. Leanne Payne, *The Broken Image: Restoring Personal Wholeness through Healing Prayer*, Baker Books, 1996, p. 135.

Chapter 7

1. Leanne Payne, *Restoring the Christian Soul*, Baker Books, 1997, pp. 198–199.
2. Penelope Lee, *The Law of Love*, Authentic Films and Videos (STL), 1989.
3. Jackie Pullinger, *Crack in the Wall*, Hodder and Stoughton, 1989; *Chasing the Dragon*, Hodder and Stoughton, 1980.

Chapter 10

1. Oswald Chambers, *My Utmost for His Highest*, Classic Edition, Barbour Publishing Inc., 1963, 17 April.

Chapter 13

1. Oswald Chambers, *My Utmost for His Highest*, Oswald Chambers Publications Association Ltd, 1992, 26 November.

Chapter 14

1. Emil Brunner, *Man in Revolt: A Christian Anthropology*, trans. O. Wyon, Lutterworth, 1939, p. 34.

Chapter 15

1. Alex G. Smith, *Buddhism through Christian Eyes*, OMF International, 2001, p. 21.

Conclusion

1. Leanne Payne, *Newsletter*, Pastoral Care Ministries, Summer, 2008.
2. Leanne Payne, *Newsletter*, Pastoral Care Ministries, Fall 2004.

Prayers and pointers for taking things further

1. Andrew Comiskey, *Pursuing Sexual and Relational Wholeness in Christ*, Desert Stream Publications, 1996, p. 26.